PRATILIPI COMICS

# THE SIKH GURUS

NANCY K. CHADHA

Published by Westland Books, a division of Nasadiya Technologies Private Limited, in 2024

No. 269/2B, First Floor, 'Irai Arul', Vimalraj Street, Nethaji Nagar, Alapakkam Main Road, Maduravoyal, Chennai 600095

Westland and the Westland logo are the trademarks of Nasadiya Technologies Private Limited, or its affiliates.



ISBN: 9789360457822

10 9 8 7 6 5 4 3 2 1



Creative Producer: Dr Rajeev Tamhankar
Art direction: Ayantika Roy
Comic script: Aleena Mary Jose
Operations lead: Angelin Diana
Art and lettering: Ayantika Roy, Vivek G. and Kathan Diwan
Quality assurance supervisor: Abhigyan Singh

Printed at Nutech Print Services, India

# Guru Nanak Dev

(1469 - 1539)

*Awwal Allah Noor Upaya Qudrat Ke Sab Bande*
*Ek Noor Te Sab Jag Upjaya Kaun Bhalle Kaun Mande*

In the beginning Allah created Light.
From that Light He created all Mortal Beings.
From the one Light, the entire Universe welled up,
so who is good and who is bad?

SIKHISM, FOUNDED BY GURU NANAK DEV IN THE 16TH CENTURY, PREACHES UNIVERSAL LOVE, EQUALITY AND DEVOTION TO ONE GOD. IT CAME ABOUT AMIDST RELIGIOUS CONFLICTS, EMPHASISING JUSTICE AND INCLUSIVITY.
ITS TEACHINGS, ROOTED IN COMPASSION AND SELFLESSNESS, UNITE PEOPLE ACROSS CASTE AND RELIGION, INSPIRING MILLIONS TO FIND THE DIVINE IN THEMSELVES AND OTHERS.

ON 16 APRIL 1469, IN TALWANDI, NOW CALLED NANKANA SAHIB, IN PRESENT-DAY PAKISTAN, A BOY WAS BORN INTO A HINDU FAMILY.
HIS PARENTS, TRIPTA AND MEHTA KALU, GAVE HIM THE NAME NANAK, WHICH RHYMED WITH NANKI, THE NAME OF HIS SISTER WHO WAS FIVE YEARS OLDER THAN HIM.
NANAK RECEIVED A TRADITIONAL EDUCATION FROM THE HINDU ASHRAM.
HE ALSO LEARNT ARITHMETIC AND PERSIAN FROM THE MUSLIM MADRASA.

HOWEVER, HE FELT THAT REAL EDUCATION MEANT THE KNOWLEDGE ABOUT GOD.
AFTER READING THE SCRIPTURES OF BOTH THE HINDU AND MUSLIM RELIGIONS, NANAK FELT THAT THERE COULD NOT BE TWO SEPARATE GODS—RAM FOR THE HINDUS AND ALLAH FOR THE MUSLIMS.
THE RAMAYANA
THE HOLY QURAN
HE BELIEVED THAT THERE IS ONLY ONE GOD WHO LOVES ALL PEOPLE EQUALLY, REGARDLESS OF THE NAME THEY USE TO CALL HIM.

ONE DAY, HIS MOTHER, MATA TRIPTA, WAS BUSY MAKING SOME SWEETS. MOTHER: NANAK, LOOK I MADE YOUR FAVOURITE SWEETS.
NANAK, LOOK I MADE YOUR FAVOURITE SWEETS.
MOTHER, CAN I TAKE THESE SWEETS TO MY FRIENDS?
MATA TRIPTA WAS VERY HAPPY. SHE TOOK PRIDE IN HER SON'S GENEROSITY.
YES, OF COURSE. THERE'S ENOUGH FOR EVERYONE.
NANAK TOOK THE SWEETS AND RAN TO HIS FRIENDS.
LOOK, WHAT I GOT! MOTHER MADE ENOUGH FOR ALL OF US!

WONDERFUL, NANAK! HOW KIND OF YOU!
I'VE EATEN MORE THAN I NEEDED TO. LET'S PLAY. I WANT TO BE IN NANAK'S TEAM.
ME TOO!
PLEASE THANK YOUR MOTHER ON OUR BEHALF.
NANAK AND HIS FRIENDS HAPPILY TOSSED THE BALL BACK AND FORTH, COMPLETELY ENGROSSED IN A LIVELY GAME OF CATCH.
AFTER A WHILE, ALL OF THEM SETTLED DOWN BY THE POND, COMPLETELY EXHAUSTED.
TAKE A MOMENT TO ADMIRE THE BEAUTY THAT SURROUNDS US, MY FRIENDS. IT'S ALL CREATED BY GOD!

AS DARKNESS FELL, NANAK GATHERED THE REMAINING SWEETS AND HEADED HOME. ON HIS WAY, HE ENCOUNTERED SOME SADHUS.
NANAK OFFERED THE REMAINING SWEETS TO THE SADHUS.
OH, THAT IS SO GENEROUS OF YOU, CHILD!
KIND-HEARTED CHILD, MAY GOD BLESS YOU.
YOU ARE ALL SUCH LEARNED MEN. PLEASE ENLIGHTEN ME: WHAT IS THE PURPOSE OF THIS LIFE THAT WE ARE LIVING?
WE ARE BORN, AND EVENTUALLY WE DIE. WHAT TRULY DEFINES THE SOUL'S JOURNEY? HAVE YOU MET GOD? HOW CAN ONE COME FACE TO FACE WITH GOD?
NANAK ASKED QUESTION AFTER QUESTION. HIS THIRST FOR KNOWLEDGE WAS UNQUENCHABLE.
ALTHOUGH THEY COULDN'T ANSWER ALL HIS QUESTIONS, THEY WERE DEEPL INTRIGUED BY HIS CURIOSITY, PARTICULARLY CONSIDERING HIS YOUNG AGE.
THIS CHILD IS SO EXTRAORDINARY. HE IS DEFINITELY THE CHILD OF GOD.

WHEN NANAK WAS ABOUT NINE YEARS OLD, HIS PARENTS SUMMONED THE FAMILY PRIEST, PANDIT HARDAYAL, TO PERFORM THE SACRED THREAD CEREMONY OR THE JANEU CEREMONY.
THE CEREMONY MARKED A YOUNG BOY'S COMING OF AGE AND THE COMMENCEMENT OF HIS FORMAL EDUCATION UNDER A MASTER'S GUIDANCE. NEIGHBOURS, RELATIVES AND FRIENDS WERE INVITED TO JOIN IN THE SOLEMN OCCASION.
JUST AS THE PRIEST WAS ABOUT TO DRAPE THE THREAD OVER HIS NECK, NANAK HALTED HIM.
WHY SHALL I WEAR THIS THREAD?
IT WILL ALWAYS REMIND YOU OF GOD.
I REMEMBER GOD ALL THE TIME. I DO NOT NEED A THREAD TO REMIND ME OF HIM.

THIS THREAD REINFORCES CASTE SUPERIORITY, SYMBOLISING ONE'S HIGH BIRTH AND STATUS. WITHOUT IT, ONE MAY BE REGARDED AS A PERSON FROM THE LOWEST CASTE.
THEN I SHALL NOT WEAR IT. IT PROMOTES INEQUALITY AMONG PEOPLE IN A SOCIETY.
PANDIT HARDAYAL'S FRUSTRATION GREW, YET MOSTLY EVERYONE ATTENDING THE CEREMONY WAS CAPTIVATED BY THE UNDENIABLE SENSIBILITY OF NANAK'S WORDS.
HIS REFUSAL TO WEAR THE SACRED THREAD WAS THE FIRST OF MANY ACTIONS BY NANAK TO CHALLENGE THE AGE-OLD RITUALS THAT WERE BEING FOLLOWED BLINDLY.

ONE DAY, AS NANAK WAS SLEEPING, A COBRA SLITHERED OUT FROM A NEARBY HOLE.
JUST THEN, RAI BULAR, A MUSLIM RAJPUT LANDLORD, HAPPENED TO PASS BY.
OH, MY GOD! THERE IS A HUGE COBRA NEAR NANAK. I MUST RESCUE HIM.
AS RAI BULAR APPROACHED, HE WAS AMAZED. HE OBSERVED THAT AS THE SUN MOVED, THE COBRA ADJUSTED ITSELF TO GIVE SHADE TO NANAK
RAI BULAR REALISED THAT THE COBRA WAS HARMLESS FOR NANAK. IT WAS ACTUALLY PROTECTING HIM FROM THE SUN'S HARSH RAYS AS HE SLEPT.
A CROWD GATHERED AND WITNESSED NANAK'S ABILITY TO INSPIRE COMPASSION EVEN IN ANIMALS, EMPHASISING THE DIVINE PRESENCE IN ALL BEINGS.

AFTER THIS INCIDENT, NANAK SPENT MOST TIME SINGING HYMNS IN THE PRAISE OF GOD AND HELPING THOSE IN NEED. HIS FATHER, HOWEVER, WANTED HIM TO LEARN BUSINESS SKILLS.
ONE DAY, MEHTA KALU DECIDED TO TEACH NANAK THE VALUE OF MONEY.
MY SON, TAKE THIS MONEY. BARGAIN FOR SOME FOOD ITEMS, THEN SELL THEM FOR A HIGHER PRICE TO MAKE A GOOD PROFIT!
I WILL TRY MY BEST, FATHER.
NANAK DID EVERYTHING AS HIS FATHER HAD INSTRUCTED HIM TO. BUT NO ONE SEEMED TO BE INTERESTED IN HIS GOODS.
I WILL TAKE A BREAK. I'LL GO TO THE POND AND MEDITATE.
HE CAME ACROSS A FEW HOLY MEN BY THE SIDE OF THE POND.
WHERE HAVE YOU COME FROM?
WE DO NOT HAVE A HOME. WE WANDER ABOUT EVERYWHERE.
WE HAVE FAITH THAT OUR GOD WILL CARE FOR US.

NANAK FELT HE WOULD BE SERVING GOD BY SERVING THE HOLY MEN. HE SELFLESSLY GAVE HIS ENTIRE PURCHASE TO THEM.
WHEN HE RETURNED HOME, HIS FATHER WAS FURIOUS. HE SLAPPED NANAK HARD.
I GAVE YOU THE MONEY TO MAKE A PROFIT.
THAP
MEHTA KALU GOT NANAK MARRIED TO SULAKHNI AT AN EARLY AGE. HE HOPED IT WOULD INSTIL A SENSE OF RESPONSIBILITY IN HIM AND ENCOURAGE HIM TO SAVE FOR HIS FAMILY'S FUTURE.
BUT NANAK STEADFASTLY HELD ONTO HIS BELIEF THAT HELPING OTHERS WAS THE TRUE TREASURE, CAUSING A RIFT BETWEEN HIM AND HIS FATHER.

ONE DAY, NANKI, NANAK'S OLDER SISTER, VISITED HIM.
NANAK, MY HUSBAND HAS ARRANGED A JOB FOR YOU AS THE MANAGER OF THE GRANARY STORES OWNED BY A NAWAB IN SULTANPUR.
DESPITE HIS NEW RESPONSIBILITIES TOWARDS HIS FAMILY, INCLUDING HIS TWO BABY SONS, NANAK CONTINUED TO GIVE ALMS GENEROUSLY AND ENGAGE IN RELIGIOUS DISCOURSES.
FINDING COMFORT IN HIS WORDS, THE PEOPLE OF SULTANPUR, SOUGHT HIS GUIDANCE.
BUT SOME PEOPLE ENVIED NANAK'S RISING FAME, GOING AS FAR AS LEVELLING FALSE CHARGES AGAINST HIM.
THE STOCKS THAT THIS MAN IS DISTRIBUTING SO FREELY ARE STOLEN FROM THE GRANARY STORES.

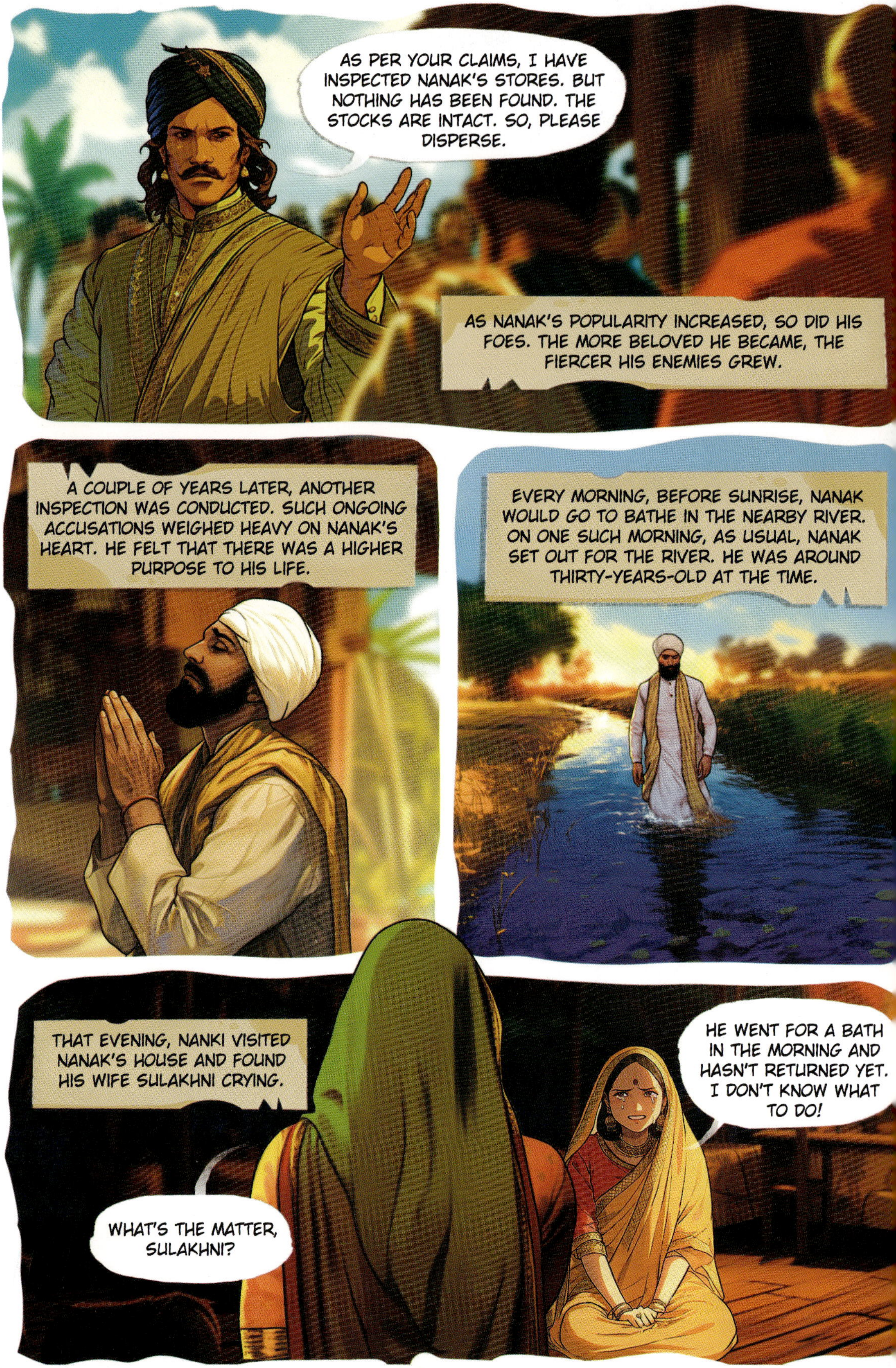
AS PER YOUR CLAIMS, I HAVE INSPECTED NANAK'S STORES. BUT NOTHING HAS BEEN FOUND. THE STOCKS ARE INTACT. SO, PLEASE DISPERSE.
AS NANAK'S POPULARITY INCREASED, SO DID HIS FOES. THE MORE BELOVED HE BECAME, THE FIERCER HIS ENEMIES GREW.
A COUPLE OF YEARS LATER, ANOTHER INSPECTION WAS CONDUCTED. SUCH ONGOING ACCUSATIONS WEIGHED HEAVY ON NANAK'S HEART. HE FELT THAT THERE WAS A HIGHER PURPOSE TO HIS LIFE.
EVERY MORNING, BEFORE SUNRISE, NANAK WOULD GO TO BATHE IN THE NEARBY RIVER. ON ONE SUCH MORNING, AS USUAL, NANAK SET OUT FOR THE RIVER. HE WAS AROUND THIRTY-YEARS-OLD AT THE TIME.
THAT EVENING, NANKI VISITED NANAK'S HOUSE AND FOUND HIS WIFE SULAKHNI CRYING.
WHAT'S THE MATTER, SULAKHNI?
HE WENT FOR A BATH IN THE MORNING AND HASN'T RETURNED YET. I DON'T KNOW WHAT TO DO!

A SEARCH PARTY WAS FORMED. FOR THREE DAYS AND NIGHTS PEOPLE FROM INSIDE AND OUTSIDE THE VILLAGE SEARCHED FOR NANAK.
BUT THEIR BELOVED NANAK WAS NOWHERE TO BE FOUND.
THERE SEEMS TO BE NO SIGN OF HIM, ANYWHERE. WE FEAR HE MAY HAVE DROWNED IN THE RIVER.
NANAK'S FAMILY WAS DEVASTATED AND THE ENTIRE VILLAGE WAS PLUNGED INTO GLOOM.
THREE DAYS AFTER HE HAD GONE MISSING, NANAK RETURNED HOME ...
OH, NANAK! YOU ARE BACK. I KNEW NOTHING HAD HAPPENED TO YOU.
WHERE DID YOU VANISH? YOUR SONS HAVEN'T STOPPED CRYING EVER SINCE.
NANAK REMAINED SILENT. HE HAD AN ETHEREAL GLOW ON HIS FACE—A RADIANCE THAT SPOKE OF A JOURNEY BEYOND THE EARTHLY REALM.

NEWS OF NANAK'S RETURN SPREAD LIKE WILDFIRE.
WHERE WERE YOU FOR THREE DAYS?
I WAS CALLED BY THE SUPREME ONE TO BRING HIS MESSAGE: 'THERE IS NO HINDU AND NO MUSALMAN. DO NOT DIVIDE PEOPLE. THEY ARE ALL CHILDREN OF THE SAME FATHER—GOD'.
WHEN THE GOVERNOR OF SULTANPUR HEARD THIS, HE WAS INFURIATED. HE CALLED FOR NANAK TO APPEAR BEFORE HIM.
HOW CAN YOU SAY THERE IS NO HINDU AND NO MUSALMAN? YOU ARE EITHER A HINDU OR A MUSLIM.
I AM NEITHER. I AM A MAN OF GOD!
THEN YOU SHOULD HAVE NO OBJECTION TO COME AND PRAY WITH US AT THE MOSQUE!
I WOULD GLADLY PRAY WITH YOU.
AT THE MOSQUE, THE QAZI LED THE PRAYER. EVERYONE GOT DOWN ON THEIR KNEES. BUT NANAK REMAINED STANDING. THIS ANGERED THE GOVERNOR AND THE QAZI.

WHY DID YOU NOT PRAY WITH US? YOU SAID YOU WOULD JOIN US IN OUR PRAYERS!
I SAID I WOULD JOIN YOU IN YOUR PRAYERS, BUT YOU WERE NOT PRAYING. THE QAZI WAS THINKING OF HIS NEWBORN COLT AND YOU WERE THINKING OF THE MONEY YOU WILL MAKE AFTER SELLING YOUR HORSES.
NANAK WAS RIGHT. THEY REALISED THAT NANAK WAS GENUINELY GIFTED AND DEEPLY CONNECTED TO GOD.
THE RIVER INCIDENT LEFT NANAK RESTLESS. HE QUIT HIS JOB, ENTRUSTED HIS WIFE AND SONS TO HIS FATHER-IN-LAW, AND SET OUT TO PREACH HIS SPIRITUAL MESSAGE. HE CONFIDED IN HIS FRIEND MARDANA, A MUSLIM MUSICIAN, WHO WAS LIKE A BROTHER TO HIM.
BHAI MARDANA, I MUST LEAVE SULTANPUR. THERE IS SO MUCH TO SHARE WITH THE WORLD—DIVERSE PATHS TO EXPLORE, CULTURES TO ENGAGE AND INJUSTICES TO CONFRONT.
NANAK INFORMED HIS FAMILY ABOUT HIS DECISION TO SPREAD THE WORD OF GOD.
THE ONE, WHO HAS LED ME TO THIS PATH, SHALL FULFIL MY DUTIES WHILE I'M GONE.
BUT WHAT ABOUT YOUR DUTIES TOWARDS YOUR FAMILY? WHO WILL LOOK AFTER ALL OF US?

NANAK AND BHAI MARDANA TRAVELLED THROUGH ROUGH TERRAIN WITH NO ROADS. DESPITE THIS, CROWDS GATHERED TO HEAR NANAK'S TEACHINGS, WHEREVER THEY WENT. THEY AFFECTIONATELY CALLED HIM BABA NANAK.
BABA NANAK AAYA ... BABA NANAK AAYA.
DURING HIS TRAVELS, BABA NANAK REACHED SAIDPUR NAGAR IN PUNJAB, WHERE HE MET A CARPENTER NAMED BHAI LALO, WHO KINDLY OFFERED THEM SHELTER IN HIS HUMBLE HOME.
I AM SORRY, MY MASTER, I HAVE ONLY THIS SIMPLE FOOD TO OFFER YOU.
BABA NANAK WAS AWARE OF MARDANA'S THOUGHTS.
I LEFT ALL THAT DELICIOUS FOOD IN SULTANPUR, AND AFTER DAYS OF JOURNEY, THIS IS WHAT I GET TO EAT!
TAKE A MORSEL! I KNOW YOU WILL ASK FOR MORE AFTER THAT.
BHAI MARDANA FINISHED EVERYTHING ON HIS PLATE AND WAS THROWING GLANCES TOWARDS THE KITCHEN IN THE HOPE FOR MORE.
YOU WERE RIGHT! THIS FOOD LOOKED SO SIMPLE, YET IT WAS SO DELICIOUS!
I KNEW YOU WOULD LOVE IT. THIS FOOD IS MADE WITH THE LOVE THAT BHAI LALO HAS IN HIS HEART. IT HAD TO BE NOTHING BUT DELICIOUS.

NEWS OF BABA NANAK'S ARRIVAL IN SAIDPUR SPREAD FAST. SOON, MALIK BHAGO, A WEALTHY OFFICER, ORGANISED A LAVISH FEAST FOR MANY HOLY PEOPLE. BABA NANAK POLITELY DECLINED HIS INVITATION, WHICH OFFENDED MALIK BHAGO.
TELL BABA NANAK THAT I WANT HIM TO COME VISIT ME. IF HE DOESN'T AGREE, BRING HIM WITH FORCE.
FINALLY, BABA NANAK VISITED MALIK BHAGO'S MANSION.
BABA NANAK, WHY DID YOU TURN DOWN MY HOSPITALITY? HOW COULD BHAI LALO'S SORRY MEAL SATIATE YOU INSTEAD OF MY SUMPTUOUS FEAST? PLEASE TELL ME.
BABA NANAK KNEW ABOUT MALIK BHAGO'S UNFAIR WAYS OF GAINING WEALTH AND POSSESSIONS. HE EXPLOITED HIS WORKERS WITHOUT ANY CARE.
HOW CAN I ENJOY A FEAST WHICH IS INFUSED WITH THE SWEAT AND BLOOD OF THE POOR?
HOW DARE YOU ACCUSE ME OF STEALING FROM MY WARDS? PROVE TO ME WHAT YOU CLAIM.
SURELY! PLEASE GIVE ME A PIECE OF SWEET FROM YOUR TABLE.

BABA NANAK REQUESTED FOR SOME SIMPLE BREAD FROM BHAI LALO'S HOUSE. HE HELD THE SWEET IN ONE HAND AND THE PLAIN BREAD IN THE OTHER, SQUEEZING BOTH.
OH! OH!
AS HE DID THAT, MILK FLOWED FROM THE DRY BREAD, WHILE DROPS OF CRIMSON BLOOD TRICKLED DOWN HIS OTHER HAND WHICH HELD THE SWEET FROM MALIK BHAGO'S TABLE.
EVERYONE IN THE ROOM WAS STUNNED BY WHAT THEY SAW.
BHAI LALO'S FOOD IS MADE WITH LOVE, WHILE YOURS IS MADE WITH FEAR AND ANGER—THE FEAR THAT YOUR SERVANTS FEEL IF SOMETHING DOES NOT TASTE RIGHT; AND ANGER FOR THE WAY YOU TREAT THEM. FOOD NOURISHES ONE ONLY WHEN MADE WITH LOVE AND DEVOTION.
I'M ASHAMED OF WHAT I'VE DONE. I'LL GIVE BACK WHAT I TOOK BY FORCE AND PLEDGE TO CARE FOR MY EMPLOYEES. PLEASE TEACH ME HOW TO BE A BETTER PERSON.
MALIK BHAGO BECAME A DEVOUT FOLLOWER OF GURU NANAK AFTER THAT INCIDENT. GURU NANAK AND BHAI MARDANA ALSO CONTINUED ON THEIR SPIRITUAL JOURNEY.

FROM SAIDPUR NAGAR, BABA NANAK AND BHAI MARDANA TRAVELLED TO HARIDWAR. THEY CAME ACROSS SOME PILGRIMS POURING WATER IN THE DIRECTION OF THE SUN WHILE BATHING IN THE GANGES.
WHAT ARE YOU DOING?
WE ARE OFFERING WATER TO THE SUN AS A TRIBUTE TO THE SPIRITS OF OUR ANCESTORS.
BABA NANAK TURNED AND BEGAN OFFERING WATER IN THE OTHER DIRECTION.
WHAT ARE YOU DOING? THE SUN IS IN THIS DIRECTION.
I AM POURING WATER IN THE DIRECTION OF MY FIELDS.
HOW SILLY! HOW CAN WATER REACH YOUR FIELDS FROM HERE?
IF YOU CAN OFFER WATER TO YOUR ANCESTORS IN HEAVEN, THEN WHY CAN'T THE WATER I OFFER REACH MY FIELDS, WHICH ARE MERELY A FEW HUNDRED KILOMETRES AWAY?
HOW ELSE DO WE SHOW REVERENCE TO OUR ANCESTORS?
FILL YOUR HEARTS WITH LOVE FOR THE DIVINE AND KEEP THE DEVOTION ALIVE IN YOUR HEART AND MIND. SERVE YOUR ELDERS, EACH OTHER AND YOUR COMMUNITY. THAT IS WHERE GOD RESIDES.

THE NEXT DAY, BABA NANAK, BHAI MARDANA AND BABA NANAK'S CHILDHOOD FRIEND BHAI BALA, A LOW-CASTE HINDU, DEPARTED FROM HARIDWAR. THEIR BOND SYMBOLISED UNITY AMONG DIVERSE COMMUNITIES.
THEY WERE CROSSING A VILLAGE TOGETHER.
MASTER, WE HAVE BEEN WALKING FOR A LONG TIME. I AM VERY THIRSTY.
GO TO THE TOP OF THIS HILL. YOU MAY FIND SOME DRINKING WATER THERE.
BHAI MARDANA WALKED UP THE HILL AND MET A MAN BY A WELL.
CAN WE PLEASE HAVE SOME WATER? MY COMPANIONS AND I ARE VERY THIRSTY.
YOU HAVE TO BUY IT. NO ONE CAN DRAW WATER FROM MY WELL UNLESS THEY PAY FOR IT.
THE MAN, WHO OWNED THE ONLY WELL IN THE VILLAGE, WAS CONCEITED AND GREEDY. KNOWING THE DIRE NEED FOR WATER IN THE VILLAGE, HE EXPLOITED THE SCARCITY FOR HIS OWN GAIN.
BHAI MARDANA CAME DOWN THE HILL AND NARRATED THE INCIDENT TO BABA NANAK.
WE MUST GIVE HIM THREE CHANCES. GO TO HIM AGAIN AND ASK FOR WATER IN THE NAME OF GOD.

BHAI MARDANA WENT TO THE MAN TWICE, BUT CAME DOWN THE HILL EMPTY-HANDED EACH TIME.
SO THE GREEDY MAN DID NOT GIVE YOU WATER, WHICH HE THINKS IS HIS? UNGRACIOUS AND IGNORANT IS THE MAN WHO DOESN'T KNOW THAT ALL THINGS THAT COME FROM GOD RETURN TO GOD. DON'T WORRY! GOD WILL TAKE CARE OF US.
BABA NANAK PICKED UP A SMALL STICK AND DUG IT INTO THE GROUND.
A SPRING OF PURE, CRYSTAL-CLEAR WATER BURST FORTH FROM THE HOLE.
OH, SO MUCH WATER!
SUCH REFRESHING WATER!
QUENCHING THEIR THIRST, THEY HAD THEIR FILL OF THE COOL SPRING WATER.

THE VILLAGERS CAME RUNNING. THEY GATHERED AROUND THE SPRING WITH POTS, EAGERLY TAKING THEIR FILL.
THE MAN AT THE TOP OF THE HILL HEARD THE COMMOTION AND PEERED DOWN TO SEE WHAT WAS GOING ON.
WHERE IS ALL THAT WATER COMING FROM? THAT TOO WHEN MY WELL HAS STARTED DRYING UP! OH, THAT BABA MUST BE BEHIND THIS. I MUST TEACH HIM A LESSON.
IN A FIT OF RAGE, HE PUSHED A BOULDER TOWARDS BABA NANAK.
PUSH
THE BOULDER WENT ROARING DOWN THE HILL, PICKING UP SPEED AS IT WENT.
THRURRR

EVERYONE EXCEPT BABA NANAK RAN OUT OF THE BOULDER'S WAY, FEARING FOR THEIR LIVES.
BABA, RUN!
BABA NANAK MADE NO ATTEMPT TO MOVE. HE SIMPLY LIFTED HIS HAND IN THE DIRECTION OF THE BOULDER.
THE HUGE BOULDER CAME TO AN ABRUPT HALT WHEN IT TOUCHED BABA NANAK'S OUTSTRETCHED HAND.
BABA NANAK, YOU ARE SAFE!
BABA NANAK'S PALM LEFT AN IMPRINT ON THE BOULDER, AS IF IT WASN'T MADE OF HARD STONE BUT OF MALLEABLE CLAY.
HOW IS THIS POSSIBLE?

WITNESSING THE MIRACLES, THE MAN PLEADED WITH BABA NANAK FOR FORGIVENESS.
GURU NANAK! GURU NANAK!
NOTHING BELONGS TO US. EVERYTHING IS A CREATION OF GOD.
FROM THAT DAY ON, THE MAN BECAME AN ARDENT DEVOTEE OF GURU NANAK.

THE BOULDER WITH THE IMPRINT OF GURU NANAK'S PALM IS INTACT IN A HOLY SHRINE CALLED PANJA SAHIB GURUDWARA NEAR ISLAMABAD IN PAKISTAN.

GURU NANAK UNDERTOOK FOUR EXTENSIVE JOURNEYS, LATER NAMED 'UDASIS', TRAVELLING ACROSS INDIA, TIBET, SRI LANKA AND THE MIDDLE EAST. HIS TEACHINGS, WHICH CAME TO BE KNOWN AS 'SAKHIS', SPREAD THE MESSAGE OF LOVE, COMPASSION AND DIVINE UNITY.

THE SAKHIS PROPAGATED THE IDEA OF ONE GOD, REJECTED EMPTY RITUALS AND INSPIRED SELFLESS SERVICE (SEWA) AND EQUALITY AMONG ALL HUMAN BEINGS REGARDLESS OF CASTE, CREED OR GENDER.

DURING ONE OF HIS JOURNEYS, GURU NANAK, ACCOMPANIED BY BHAI MARDANA, REACHED MECCA, THE MOST SACRED PLACE OF WORSHIP FOR MUSLIMS. EXHAUSTED UPON ARRIVAL, GURU NANAK DECIDED TO REST.
WHEN HE SLEPT, HIS FEET HAPPENED TO POINT TOWARDS THE KAABA, THE MOST REVERED SHRINE OF THE MUSLIMS. IT'S CONSIDERED IMPROPER, AS MUSLIMS WORLDWIDE PRAY IN THAT DIRECTION.
WHY ARE YOU SLEEPING WITH YOUR FEET POINTING TOWARDS KAABA? THIS IS UTTER DISRESPECT!
FORGIVE ME, BROTHERS. IF YOU BELIEVE I HAVE DISRESPECTED THE HOUSE OF GOD, THEN PLEASE TURN MY FEET IN THE DIRECTION WHERE GOD IS NOT PRESENT.
EVERYONE FELL SILENT.
WHEREVER GURU NANAK WENT, HE ESTABLISHED A 'SANGAT', A CONGREGATION IN WHICH ALL KINDS OF PEOPLE, REGARDLESS OF THEIR SOCIAL STANDING, SAT TOGETHER AS EQUALS AND SANG IN PRAISE OF GOD.

HE ALSO INTRODUCED THE CONCEPT OF 'PANGAT', WHERE EVERYONE SAT AND ATE MEALS TOGETHER, REGARDLESS OF THEIR RELIGION, CASTE OR STATUS.
HE INITIATED THE PRACTICE OF 'LANGAR', OFFERING FREE FOOD TO ALL.
GURU NANAK WAS TROUBLED BY THE BLIND ADHERENCE TO RELIGIOUS BELIEFS AND THE UNEQUAL STATUS OF WOMEN IN SOCIETY.
'SO KYUN MANDA AAKHIYE JITT JAMEIN RAAJAAN ...' HOW CAN WOMEN BE REGARDED AS INFERIOR WHEN THEY GIVE BIRTH TO ALL MEN, INCLUDING THE KINGS BEFORE WHOM PEOPLE BOW THEIR HEADS?

AS GURU NANAK AGED, HE UNDERSTOOD THE NEED FOR A SUCCESSOR TO CARRY ON HIS SPIRITUAL LEGACY. DESPITE HIS LOVE FOR HIS SONS, SRI CHAND AND LAKHMI DAS, HE BELIEVED THAT SPIRITUAL LEADERSHIP SHOULD BE BASED ON MERIT, NOT FAMILY TIES.
SO, IN 1539, HE CHOSE BHAI LEHNA, FOR HIS HONESTY AND SPIRITUAL INSIGHT. HE RENAMED HIM GURU ANGAD.
AT THE AGE OF 70, ON 22 SEPTEMBER 1539, IN KARTARPUR, GURU NANAK ASCENDED TO THE OTHER WORLD.
GURU NANAK DEDICATED HIS LIFE TO UNITING HINDUS AND MUSLIMS, REPAIRING THE FRACTURED BONDS OF BROTHERHOOD. REVERED BY BOTH COMMUNITIES, HE WAS KNOWN AS 'NANAK SHAH FAKIR', THE GURU OF HINDUS AND THE PIR OF MUSLIMS.
UPON GURU NANAK'S PASSING, HINDUS AND MUSLIMS DISPUTED OVER HIS BODY, EACH WANTING TO PERFORM THEIR RESPECTIVE RITUALS OF CREMATION OR BURIAL. HOWEVER, WHEN THEY LOOKED UNDER THE SHROUD, THEY DISCOVERED A PILE OF FLOWERS INSTEAD OF HIS BODY.

THEY DIVIDED THE SHROUD INTO TWO EQUAL PARTS AND PERFORMED THEIR SEPARATE RITUALS.
EVEN AFTER HIS PASSING, GURU NANAK'S MESSAGE CONTINUED TO LIVE ON: DO NOT DIVIDE PEOPLE BASED ON FAITH OR CASTE. LOVE WITHOUT DISCRIMINATION IS THE HIGHEST RELIGION.
TO THIS DAY, A GURUDWARA AND A MOSQUE COEXIST IN KARTARPUR.
GURU NANAK TAUGHT THAT THE PATH TO THE DIVINE IS PAVED NOT WITH RITUALS AND MEANINGLESS TRADITIONS, BUT WITH THE EARNEST DEVOTION OF A HEART ABLAZE WITH LOVE.

# Guru Angad Dev

(1504 - 1552)

*Andhhae Eaehi N Aakheean Jin Mukh Loein Naahi*
*Andhhae Saeee Naanakaa Khasamahu Ghuthhae Jaahi*

They, who have no eyes in their face, are not called blind.
They alone are blind, O Nanak, who stray away from their Lord.

GURU ANGAD WAS BORN ON 31 MARCH 1504, IN THE VILLAGE OF MATTE DI SARAI (IN PRESENT-DAY PAKISTAN) TO BHAI PHERU MAL AND MATA RAMO.
WE WILL NAME HIM LEHNA.
AT THE AGE OF SIXTEEN, HE WAS MARRIED TO A GIRL NAMED KHIVI WITH WHOM HE HAD TWO SONS, DASU AND DATU, AND TWO DAUGHTERS, AMRO AND ANOKHI.
GURU ANGAD ADOPTED AND FORMALISED THE SIKH SCRIPT, GURMUKHI. HE COMPILED GURU NANAK'S HYMNS, COLLECTIVELY KNOWN AS SHABADS AND ADDING HIS OWN COMPOSITIONS TO THE SACRED SCRIPTURE, CREATED THE FOUNDATION OF THE HOLY 'GURU GRANTH SAHIB'.
AT THE AGE OF TWENTY-SEVEN, BHAI LEHNA HEARD THE RECITATIONS OF GURU NANAK FROM HIS DISCIPLE BHAI JODHA AND DECIDED TO TRAVEL TO KARTARPUR TO MEET THE GURU.
KIND SIR, PLEASE TELL ME THE WAY TO THE GURU'S HOUSE.
GO TO THAT GATE! YOU WILL FIND THE ONE YOU WANT TO MEET.

UPON ENTERING THE ATE, BHAI LEHNA WAS STUNNED.
OH! I JUST SAW YOU OUTSIDE AND YOU ARE ... I AM SO MORTIFIED.
DON'T BE. YOU ARE MY GUEST.
BHAI LEHNA WAS DEEPLY IMPRESSED BY GURU NANAK'S HUMILITY. THEY TALKED FOR HOURS, DISCUSSING THE TRUE CREATOR AND HIS CREATIONS. FINALLY, HE DECIDED TO BECOME A SIKH.
HE STAYED ON IN KARTARPUR FOR SEVEN LONG YEARS, LEARNING AND PRACTISING THE PRINCIPLES OF THE SIKH FAITH.
YOUR DEDICATION IS COMMENDABLE. I BESTOW UPON YOU THE NAME ANGAD, WHICH MEANS, 'PART OF THE BODY'. NOW, YOU ARE A PART OF ME, CARRYING ON MY WORK. I ALSO NAME YOU AS MY SUCCESSOR.

AFTER GURU NANAK'S PASSING, GURU ANGAD LEFT FOR KHADUR SAHIB VILLAGE, FOLLOWING GURU NANAK'S TEACHING OF HONEST LABOUR (KIRAT KARO) ...
SHARING WITH THE NEEDY (VAND CHAKKO) ...
AND MEDITATING ON GOD'S NAME (NAAM JAPO).
HE ESTABLISHED CENTRES FOR PREACHING GURU NANAK'S TEACHINGS. SIKHS BEGAN MEETING THERE. THESE CENTRES THEN EVOLVED INTO GURUDWARAS.
GURU ANGAD INTRODUCED THE GURMUKHI SCRIPT THAT WAS USED TO WRITE THE SACRED SIKH SCRIPTURE, GURU GRANTH SAHIB, IN WHICH HE COMPILED THE HYMNS AND WRITINGS OF GURU NANAK.
GURU ANGAD TRAVELLED EXTENSIVELY, ESTABLISHING SEVERAL CENTRES TO PREACH SIKHISM AND TEACH GURMUKHI. HE OPENED MANY SCHOOL'S TO EDUCATE CHILDREN, AND INITIATED GURU KA LANGAR.
HIS WIFE, MAT
KHIVI, PLAYED
PIVOTAL ROL
IN THIS SEW
BY PERSONAL
PREPARING A
SERVING MEA
TO THE VISITO

GURU ANGAD INTRODUCED THE TRADITION OF 'MALL AKHARA', WHERE WRESTLING MATCHES WERE HELD TO PROMOTE PHYSICAL ACTIVITIES AND WELL-BEING.
A HEALTHY MIND LIVES IN A HEALTHY BODY. I WANT ALL OF YOU TO DEDICATEDLY ATTEND THESE AKHARAS.

HE HELD SANGAT GATHERINGS ...
GURUJI, WHAT ABOUT CASTE DIFFERENCES?
IN GOD'S EYES, ALL ARE EQUAL!

GURU ANGAD FELT THAT RELIGION WAS A WAY OF LIFE.
HOW CAN WE SERVE GOD?
TO SERVE GOD, YOU NEED TO SERVE ALL THOSE AROUND YOU. SERVE THEM WITH A SELFLESS HEART. ONE NEEDS TO CONTROL GREED.

DURING THIS PERIOD, THE THEN EMPEROR OF INDIA, HUMAYUN, WAS DEFEATED AND DETHRONED BY SHER SHAH. HUMAYUN FLED TO DELHI AND LATER TO LAHORE.
I NEED A SPIRITUAL GUIDE WHOSE BLESSINGS WILL HELP ME RETURN AS THE EMPEROR. BUT WHERE WILL I FIND SUCH A PERSON?

IT WAS WITH GURU NANAK'S BLESSINGS THAT MY FATHER HAD ACHIEVED GREAT SUCCESS. I MUST REQUEST HIM TO PRAY FOR ME.
YOUR MAJESTY, GURU NANAK'S RADIANCE HAS MOVED TO THE REALM BEYOND. GURU ANGAD HAS TAKEN HIS PLACE AT KHADUR.
THEN LET'S LEAVE TOMORROW FOR KHADUR WITH GIFTS FOR THE GURU.
UPON HIS ARRIVAL, HUMAYUN REMAINED SEATED ON HIS HORSE, WAITING FOR THE GURU TO RISE AND GREET HIM. HOWEVER, GURU ANGAD, OBLIVIOUS TO HUMAYUN'S PRESENCE, REMAINED IMMERSED IN MEDITATION.
DOES HE NOT RECOGNISE ME? IS THIS HOW A MERE FAKIR TREATS AN EMPEROR? I SHALL PUNISH HIM FOR DISRESPECTING ME.
HUMAYUN DREW HIS SWORD, INTENDING TO CUT OFF GURU ANGAD'S HEAD.
OH, EMPEROR, YOU DRAW YOUR SWORD SO READILY TO HARM SPIRITUAL BEINGS, BUT AGAINST YOUR ENEMY, SHER SHAH, YOUR SWORD FALTERED.

HUMAYUN INSTANTLY RECOGNISED GURU ANGAD'S DIVINITY.
OH, HOLY MAN OF GOD, I ASK FOR YOUR FORGIVENESS. IN MY FERVOUR, I LOST SIGHT OF THE PURPOSE OF MY VISIT. I SEEK YOUR BLESSINGS, GURU-JI. PRAY FOR ME SO THAT I MAY REGAIN MY THRONE.
I SHALL PRAY FOR YOU. YOU WILL RECLAIM YOUR KINGDOM IN DUE TIME. BUT ALWAYS KEEP THE LOVE OF GOD IN YOUR HEART. AND NEVER FORGET TO BE JUST AND KIND.
THANK YOU, REVERED GURU.
TRUE TO THE GURU'S WORDS, HUMAYUN EVENTUALLY REGAINED HIS THRONE.
URU ANGAD SERVED AS THE SECOND GURU FOR HIRTEEN YEARS UNTIL HIS PASSING ON 29 MARCH 1552, AT THE AGE OF ORTY-EIGHT. BEFORE HIS PASSING, JUST LIKE HIS GURU, HE CHOSE TO POINT HIS DISCIPLE BABA AMAR DAS AS HIS UCCESSOR, RATHER THAN HIS OWN SON.
GURU ANGAD'S TEACHINGS BRIDGED DIVIDES. HIS LEGACY LIVES ON, REMINDING US TO EMBRACE LOVE, COMPASSION AND UNITY IN OUR LIVES.

# Guru Amar Das

(1479 - 1574)

*Guru Amar Das Jinne Sevio*
*Tinne Dukh Dard Parhar Parre*

Those who serve Guru Amar Das,
their pains and poverty are taken away, far away.

ON 5 MAY 1479, IN BASARKE, PUNJAB, BHAI AMAR DAS WAS BORN. HE WAS THE ELDEST SON OF SRI TEJ BHAN AND MATA LACHMI.
AT THE AGE OF TWENTY-FOUR, HE MARRIED MANSA DEVI. HE HAD FOUR CHILDREN–TWO SONS NAMED BHAI MOHAN AND BHASI MOHRI AND TWO DAUGHTERS, BIBI DANI-JI AND BIBI BHANI-JI.
AN ENCOUNTER WITH BIBI AMRO, THE DAUGHTER OF GURU ANGAD, INSPIRED BHAI AMAR DAS TO LEARNABOUT SIKHISM.
COME, LET ME TAKE YOU TO MY FATHER. HE WILL GUIDE YOU IN THE WAYS OF SIKHISM.
BHAI AMAR DAS EMBRACED SIKHISM AT THE AGE OF SIXTY-ONE UNDER THE GUIDANCE OF GURU ANGAD. HE THEN MOVED TO KHADUR SAHIB TO SERVE GURU ANGAD.

BHAI AMAR DAS ENSURED GURU ANGAD'S COMFORT, EVEN ARRANGING FOR HIS BATHING ROUTINE. EACH MORNING, RAIN OR SHINE, HE FETCHED WATER FOR GURU ANGAD'S BATH FROM THE BEAS RIVER.
THE VILLAGERS NICKNAMED BHAI AMAR DAS 'AMRU'. THEY OFTEN MOCKED HIM WHILE HE WAS ON ERRANDS.
THERE GOES AMRU, THE WATER CARRIER!
DESPITE FACING RIDICULE, BHAI AMAR DAS FAITHFULLY SERVED GURU ANGAD FOR TWELVE YEARS.
ONE STORMY NIGHT ...
I AM THIRSTY. CAN SOMEONE BRING ME WATER?
THERE'S NO WATER IN THE HOUSE. IT'S TOO DARK AND STORMY OUTSIDE.
WE DON'T WANT TO GO OUT IN THIS WEATHER.
UPON HEARING THIS, BHAI AMAR DAS CAME TO ATTEND TO THE GURU.
ALLOW ME, GURU-JI. SERVING YOU UPLIFTS MY SPIRIT.

DESPITE THE STORM AND GURU ANGAD'S WARNINGS, BHAI AMAR DAS VENTURED TO THE RIVER. HE BRAVED THE RAIN AND DARKNESS, RECITING HIS MORNING PRAYERS, THE 'JAPJI SAHIB', ALONG THE WAY.
WHEN HE WAS RETURNING, HE STUMBLED AND FELL.
HEARING THE NOISE BY THE RIVERSIDE, A WEAVER AND HIS WIFE PEERED THROUGH THEIR WINDOW. THEY SAW BHAI AMAR DAS ON AN ERRAND TO GET WATER FOR THE GURU.
TELL ME, AMRU, WHAT KIND OF GURU WOULD MAKE A SEVENTY-THREE-YEAR-OLD MAN RUN ERRANDS IN A WILD STORM LIKE THIS? HE MUST BE CRAZY!
DEAR LADY, THERE MUST BE SOMETHING WRONG WITH YOU! THAT IS THE ONLY REASON YOU WOULD SPEAK THIS WAY ABOUT GURU-JI.
THE WEAVER'S WIFE'S MENTAL STATE INDEED DETERIORATED AFTER INSULTING BHAI AMAR DAS. SHE WAS OFTEN HEARD BABBLING IN AN INCOMPREHENSIBLE LANGUAGE.
BOODE ZIPPITY GORP SPLONK WOZZLE DUTLP.

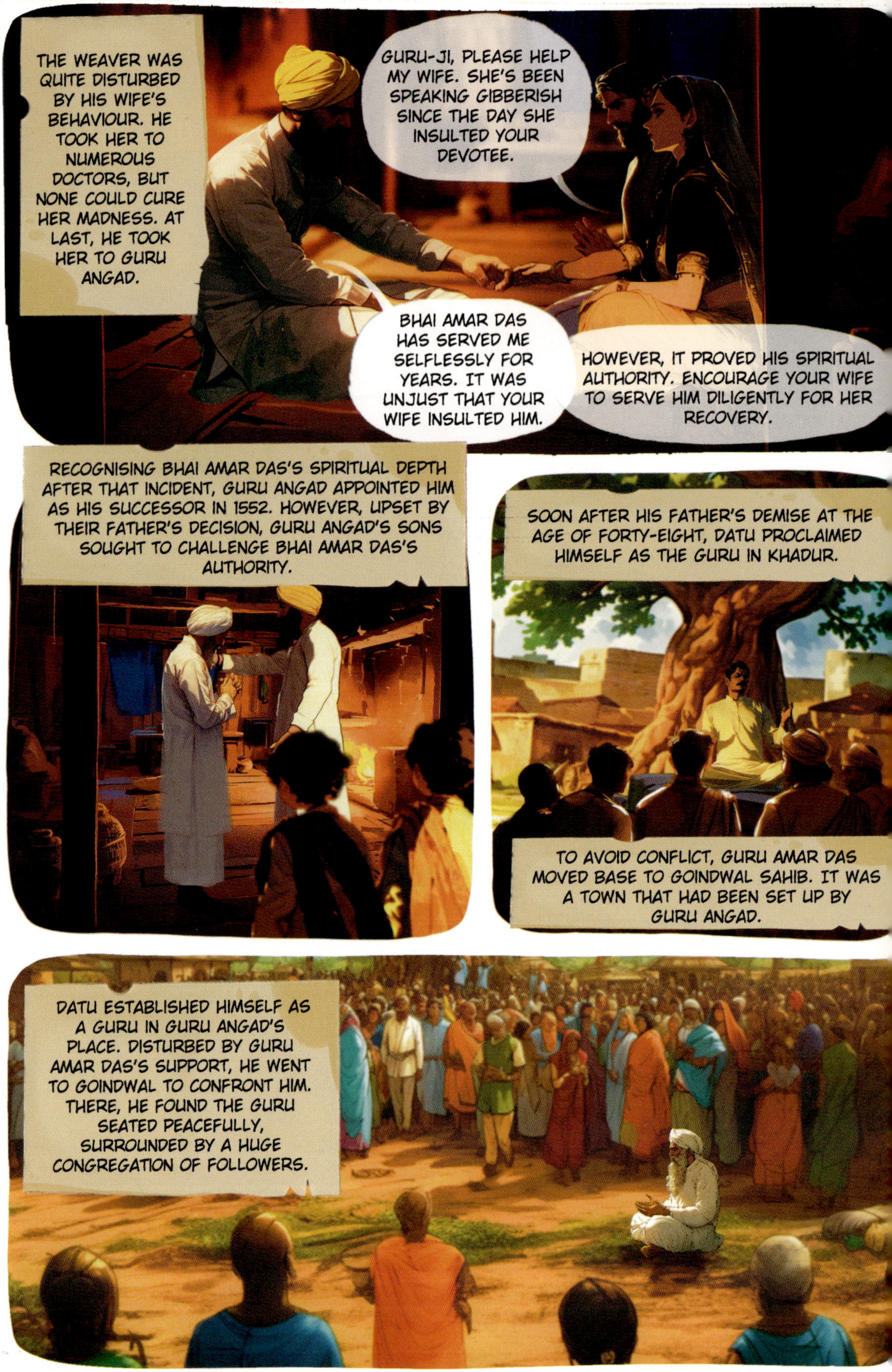
THE WEAVER WAS QUITE DISTURBED BY HIS WIFE'S BEHAVIOUR. HE TOOK HER TO NUMEROUS DOCTORS, BUT NONE COULD CURE HER MADNESS. AT LAST, HE TOOK HER TO GURU ANGAD.
GURU-JI, PLEASE HELP MY WIFE. SHE'S BEEN SPEAKING GIBBERISH SINCE THE DAY SHE INSULTED YOUR DEVOTEE.
BHAI AMAR DAS HAS SERVED ME SELFLESSLY FOR YEARS. IT WAS UNJUST THAT YOUR WIFE INSULTED HIM.
HOWEVER, IT PROVED HIS SPIRITUAL AUTHORITY. ENCOURAGE YOUR WIFE TO SERVE HIM DILIGENTLY FOR HER RECOVERY.
RECOGNISING BHAI AMAR DAS'S SPIRITUAL DEPTH AFTER THAT INCIDENT, GURU ANGAD APPOINTED HIM AS HIS SUCCESSOR IN 1552. HOWEVER, UPSET BY THEIR FATHER'S DECISION, GURU ANGAD'S SONS SOUGHT TO CHALLENGE BHAI AMAR DAS'S AUTHORITY.
SOON AFTER HIS FATHER'S DEMISE AT THE AGE OF FORTY-EIGHT, DATU PROCLAIMED HIMSELF AS THE GURU IN KHADUR.
TO AVOID CONFLICT, GURU AMAR DAS MOVED BASE TO GOINDWAL SAHIB. IT WAS A TOWN THAT HAD BEEN SET UP BY GURU ANGAD.
DATU ESTABLISHED HIMSELF AS A GURU IN GURU ANGAD'S PLACE. DISTURBED BY GURU AMAR DAS'S SUPPORT, HE WENT TO GOINDWAL TO CONFRONT HIM. THERE, HE FOUND THE GURU SEATED PEACEFULLY, SURROUNDED BY A HUGE CONGREGATION OF FOLLOWERS.

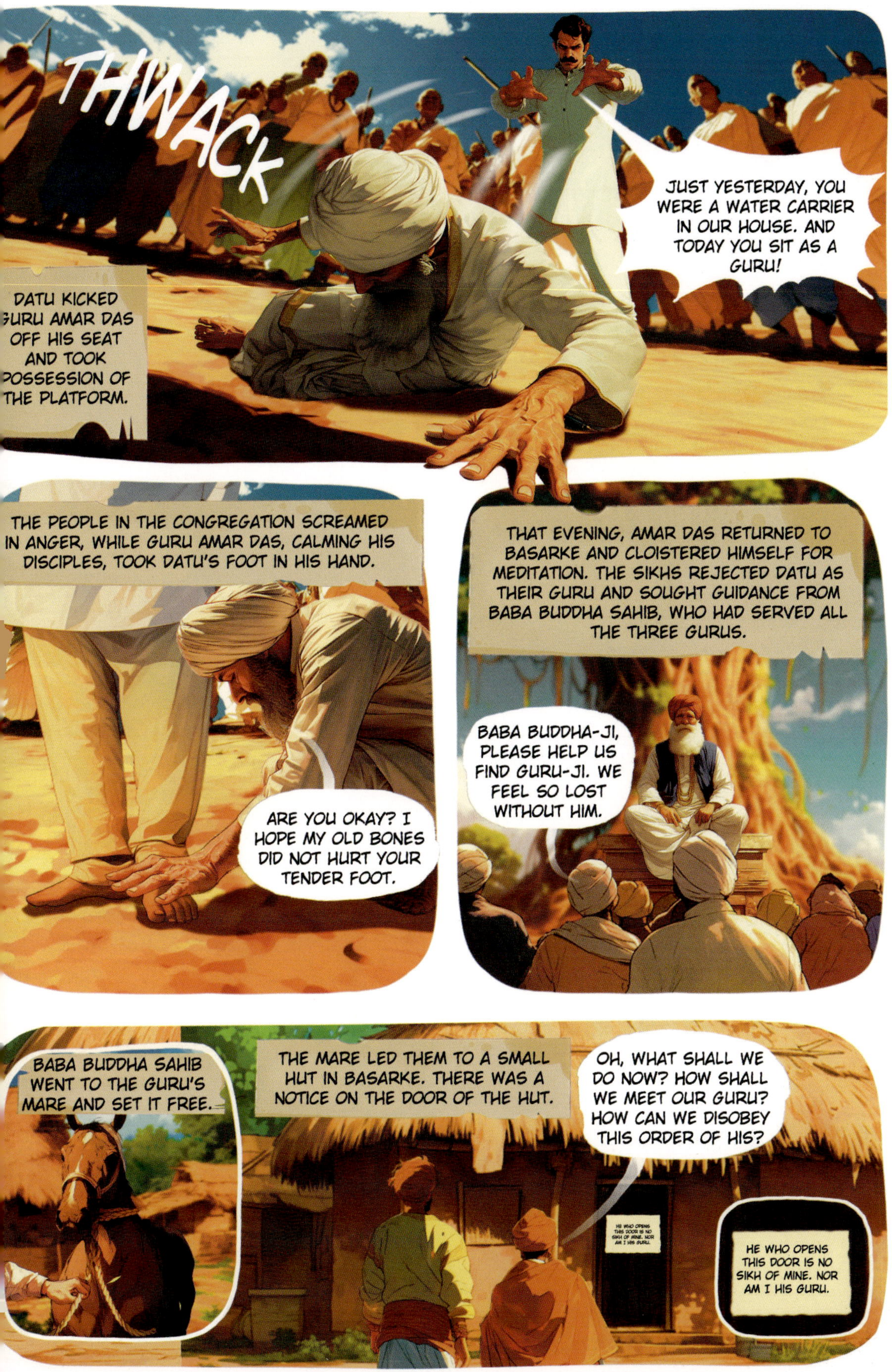
THWACK
JUST YESTERDAY, YOU WERE A WATER CARRIER IN OUR HOUSE. AND TODAY YOU SIT AS A GURU!
DATU KICKED GURU AMAR DAS OFF HIS SEAT AND TOOK POSSESSION OF THE PLATFORM.
THE PEOPLE IN THE CONGREGATION SCREAMED IN ANGER, WHILE GURU AMAR DAS, CALMING HIS DISCIPLES, TOOK DATU'S FOOT IN HIS HAND.
ARE YOU OKAY? I HOPE MY OLD BONES DID NOT HURT YOUR TENDER FOOT.
THAT EVENING, AMAR DAS RETURNED TO BASARKE AND CLOISTERED HIMSELF FOR MEDITATION. THE SIKHS REJECTED DATU AS THEIR GURU AND SOUGHT GUIDANCE FROM BABA BUDDHA SAHIB, WHO HAD SERVED ALL THE THREE GURUS.
BABA BUDDHA-JI, PLEASE HELP US FIND GURU-JI. WE FEEL SO LOST WITHOUT HIM.
BABA BUDDHA SAHIB WENT TO THE GURU'S MARE AND SET IT FREE.
THE MARE LED THEM TO A SMALL HUT IN BASARKE. THERE WAS A NOTICE ON THE DOOR OF THE HUT.
OH, WHAT SHALL WE DO NOW? HOW SHALL WE MEET OUR GURU? HOW CAN WE DISOBEY THIS ORDER OF HIS?
HE WHO OPENS THIS DOOR IS NO SIKH OF MINE. NOR AM I HIS GURU.

THEY CAME UP WITH THE IDEA OF MAKING A HOLE IN THE WALL TO REACH THEIR GURU. UPON SEEING THEIR HEADS PEEPING THROUGH THE HOLE, GURU AMAR DAS EMERGED FROM HIS MEDITATION AND BEGAN LAUGHING.
YOU HAVE OUTSMARTED ME! HOW DID YOU EVEN MANAGE TO FIND ME?
GURU AMAR DAS'S RETURN WAS CELEBRATED WITH JOY AND FESTIVITY IN GOINDWAL.
HE CONSTRUCTED A WELL, THE BAOLI, TO PROVIDE WATER TO THE PEOPLE. IT HAS EIGHTY-FOUR STEPS DESCENDING TO THE BANKS OF THE BEAS RIVER. THE BAOLI BECAME A SITE OF PILGRIMAGE, AND A GURUDWARA KNOWN AS THE GOINDWAL BAOLI GURUDWARA WAS BUILT NEARBY.
GURU AMAR DAS COMPOSED A HYMN, 'ANAND SAHIB', THE SONG OF JOY. IT IS A MASTERPIECE OF SPIRITUAL POETRY, CONSISTING OF FORTY VERSES. IT CELEBRATES FREEDOM FROM SUFFERING AND ANXIETY, AND THE ATTAINMENT OF A BLISSFUL EXISTENCE .

FOLLOWING GURU NANAK'S TEACHINGS, GURU AMAR DAS CHAMPIONED EQUAL PARTICIPATION OF WOMEN IN PLACES OF WORSHIP, EDUCATION AND IN SOCIETY.
OF WOMEN WE ARE BORN, BY WOMEN CONCEIVED, TO WOMEN ENGAGED, TO WOMEN MARRIED. ONE FORMS FRIENDSHIPS WITH WOMEN; THROUGH WOMEN,GENERATIONS ARE BORN. SO WHY SHOULD WE SPEAK ILL OF THEM, WHEN, FROM THEM, KINGS ARE BORN?
GURU AMAR DAS OPPOSED THE PURDAH' SYSTEM AND ADVOCATED FOR THE DISSOLUTION OF THE PRACTICE OF SATI. HE ALSO DISAPPROVED OF THE CUSTOM OF WIDOWS REMAINING UNMARRIED FOR LIFE.
GURU AMAR DAS FIRST CONCEIVED THE IDEA OF THE SRI HARMANDIR SAHIB GURUDWARA, ALSO KNOWN AS THE GOLDEN TEMPLE, IN AMRITSAR. HE ENVISIONED AN OPEN-TO-ALL WATER BODY CALLED THE AMRIT SAROVAR, WITH THE TEMPLE AT ITS CENTRE.
THIS SACRED SITE SYMBOLISES EQUALITY AND UNITY AMONG PEOPLE OF ALL BACKGROUNDS AND FAITHS. IT BECAME SIKHISM'S MOST SACRED PILGRIMAGE DESTINATION.
AFTER TWENTY-TWO YEARS OF SERVICE, GURU AMAR DAS PEACEFULLY DEPARTED AT THE AGE OF NINETY-FIVE ON 1 SEPTEMBER 1574, IN GOINDWAL, LEAVING BEHIND A LEGACY OF LOVE AND SERVICE TO HUMANITY.

# Guru Ram Das

(1534 - 1581)

*Ramdas Sarovar Naate, Sab Uttere Paap Kamaate*

By taking a dip in the pond of Lord Ramdas, all sins are washed away.

GURU RAM DAS WAS BORN IN LAHORE IN 1534 TO BHAI HARI DAS AND MATA ANUP DEVI. HE WAS CALLED 'JETHA', MEANING 'THE FIRST BORN'.
ORPHANED AT THE AGE OF SEVEN, BHAI JETHA MADE A LIVING BY SELLING BOILED GRAINS. DESPITE HIS POVERTY, HE GENEROUSLY SHARED THE GRAINS WITH THOSE IN NEED, GIVING THEM AWAY FOR FREE.
AT THE AGE OF TWELVE, BHAI JETHA WAS INTRODUCED TO SIKHISM BY GURU AMAR DAS. IMPRESSED WITH HIS DEVOTION, GURU AMAR DAS LATER ARRANGED THE MARRIAGE OF HIS DAUGHTER, BIBI BHANI, WITH BHAI JETHA AND NAMED HIM RAM DAS, MEANING 'SERVANT OF GOD'.
GURU RAM DAS IS RENOWNED FOR FOUNDING AMRITSAR, THE SPIRITUAL EPICENTRE OF SIKHISM.
HE COMPOSED MANY HYMNS INCLUDED IN THE 'GURU GRANTH SAHIB', WHICH FOCUSED ON THEMES LIKE LOVE, DEVOTION, HUMILITY AND CONNECTING WITH THE DIVINE.

ONE DAY, GURU RAM DAS'S FIRST COUSIN, SAHARI MAL, CAME VISITING FROM LAHORE.
GURU-JI, MY SON IS GETTING MARRIED SOON. WILL YOU PLEASE COME AND BLESS THE WEDDING?
I WOULD LOVE TO, BROTHER, BUT I CANNOT LEAVE MY DUTIES IN AMRITSAR AT THE MOMENT. DON'T WORRY, I WILL SEND ONE OF MY SONS INSTEAD.
GURU RAM DAS'S TWO SONS, PRITHI CHAND AND MAHADEV, REFUSED TO GO. HE LOOKED AT HIS THIRD SON, ARJANMAL.
FATHER, I WILL GO WHEREVER YOU WISH ME TO.
THANK YOU, MY DEAR SON. BE PREPARED TO STAY FOR A WHILE AFTER THE WEDDING. I WOULD LIKE YOU TO LEAD SPIRITUAL DISCOURSES THERE.
PRITHI CHAND WAS PLEASED TO HEAR THAT ARJANMAL WAS LEAVING FOR LAHORE. NOTING HIS FATHER'S BIAS TOWARDS ARJANMAL DUE TO HIS DEDICATION AND HUMILITY, PRITHI CHAND SAW THIS AS AN OPPORTUNITY TO PERSUADE HIS FATHER TO CHOOSE HIM AS THE NEXT GURU.
ARJANMAL STAYED ON IN LAHORE AFTER THE WEDDING, CONDUCTING DISCOURSES. LATER, HE SENT A MESSENGER WITH A LETTER TO HIS FATHER EXPRESSING A DESIRE TO RETURN TO AMRITSAR AND SERVE GURU RAM DAS.
WHAT ARE GURU-JI'S ORDERS FOR ME?
GURU-JI WISHES FOR YOU TO STAY IN LAHORE TILL HE SENDS FOR YOU.

THREE YEARS PASSED. ARJANMAL'S SECOND LETTER RECEIVED THE SAME REPLY. HE THEN WROTE A THIRD LETTER TO HIS FATHER.
GIVE THIS LETTER TO GURU-JI PERSONALLY. DO NOT HAND IT OVER TO ANYONE ELSE. THIS IS A STRICT ORDER.
THE MESSENGER DID AS HE WAS INSTRUCTED.
AH, A LETTER FROM ARJANMAL AT LAST! I WAS WONDERING WHEN HE WOULD START MISSING ME. BUT WHY IS THIS MARKED AS #3? WHERE ARE THE OTHER LETTERS? I NEVER RECEIVED THEM!
GURU-JI, I GAVE THEM TO PRITHI CHAND-JI TO HAND OVER TO YOU. EACH TIME, HE INSTRUCTED ME TO ASK ARJANMAL-JI TO STAY ON UNTIL YOU CALLED FOR HIM.
GURU RAM DAS CALLED FOR HIS FIRST SON.
SON, DID YOU RECEIVE TWO LETTERS FROM THIS MESSENGER? IF SO, WHY DIDN'T YOU GIVE THEM TO ME?
LETTERS? I ... OH, YES, FATHER, I CAME TO YOU, BUT YOU WERE SO BUSY. I THOUGHT I WOULD GIVE THEM TO YOU LATER, BUT I FORGOT.
WELL, I AM NOT BUSY NOW. PLEASE BRING THEM TO ME THIS MINUTE!
FATHER, I CANNOT RECALL WHERE I KEPT THEM.

GURU RAM DAS'S ATTENDANTS SEARCHED PRITHI CHAND'S ROOM AND LOCATED BOTH THE LETTERS. THE GURU FELT DEEPLY TOUCHED AFTER READING THEM.
THIS CONFIRMED HIS SUSPICIONS ABOUT PRITHI CHAND'S UNTRUSTWORTHINESS, PROVING THAT HE WAS CLEARLY UNSUITABLE TO BE THE NEXT GURU.
THE GURU REQUESTED THE MESSENGER TO REPORT TO ARJANMAL TO RETURN TO HIM IMMEDIATELY. ARJANMAL CAME RUNNING TO HIS FATHER AND HUGGED HIM.
OH FATHER, HOW I MISSED YOU. I WILL SERVE YOU, LIVING BESIDE YOU, TILL THE END OF MY DAYS. PLEASE DON'T SEND ME AWAY FROM YOU AGAIN.
MY SON, I AM SO SORRY YOU HAD TO STAY AWAY FROM ME FOR SO LONG.
GURU RAM DAS IMMEDIATELY PLACED ARJANMAL ON HIS OWN SEAT. HE THEN HANDED AN OFFERING TO HIS SON.
I WOULD LIKE YOU TO BE THE GURU AFTER ME. PEOPLE WILL LOVE YOU AND WILL CALL YOU GURU ARJAN.
MAHADEV ACCEPTED HIS FATHER'S DECISION, BUT PRITHI CHAND COULDN'T. HE BEGAN MISTREATING HIS BROTHER ARJANMAL, PROMPTING GURU RAM DAS TO PUBLICLY CONDEMN PRITHI CHAND'S ACTIONS.
GURU RAM DAS REMEMBERED GURU AMAR DAS'S WISH TO CREATE A PILGRIMAGE SITE FOR SIKHS. HE FOUND A SPOT WITH A POOL AND DECIDED TO BUILD A LARGE TANK WITH A TEMPLE IN THE CENTRE. THE CONSTRUCTION BEGAN IN 1577 UNDER BABA BUDDHA SAHIB'S SUPERVISION.

A CITY CALLED RAMDASPUR GREW AROUND IT. GURU RAM DAS ASKED HAZRAT MIAN MIR, A MUSLIM SUFI, TO LAY THE CORNERSTONE OF HARMANDIR SAHIB, A GURUDWARA PROMOTING SIKHISM.
GURU RAM DAS INVITED TRADERS AND ARTISANS FROM FIFTY-TWO PROFESSIONS TO BOOST BUSINESS AND FUND CONSTRUCTION. THIS TRANSFORMED RAMDASPUR INTO A MAJOR COMMERCIAL CENTRE IN NORTHERN INDIA.
LATER, IT WAS RENAMED AMRITSAR, MEANING 'POOL OF NECTAR' IN PUNJABI. IT REFERS TO THE SACRED POOL SURROUNDING THE GOLDEN TEMPLE.
AMRITSAR SOON BECAME RENOWNED FOR THE HEALING PROPERTIES OF ITS SAROVAR. VISITORS DISCOVERED THAT BATHING IN ITS SACRED WATERS CURED VARIOUS AILMENTS.
MEANWHILE, THE RAJA OF MULTAN HAD BEEN SUFFERING FROM A LINGERING ILLNESS. NO DOCTOR WAS ABLE TO CURE HIM. WITH TIME, HIS CONDITION BECAME CRITICAL, AND THERE WAS NO HOPE OF RECOVERY.
IS THERE NO ONE WHO CAN HEAL ME?
I HAVE HEARD THAT WHOEVER GOES TO AMRITSAR AND TAKES A DIP IN ITS HOLY WATERS IS CURED OF ALL DISEASES.

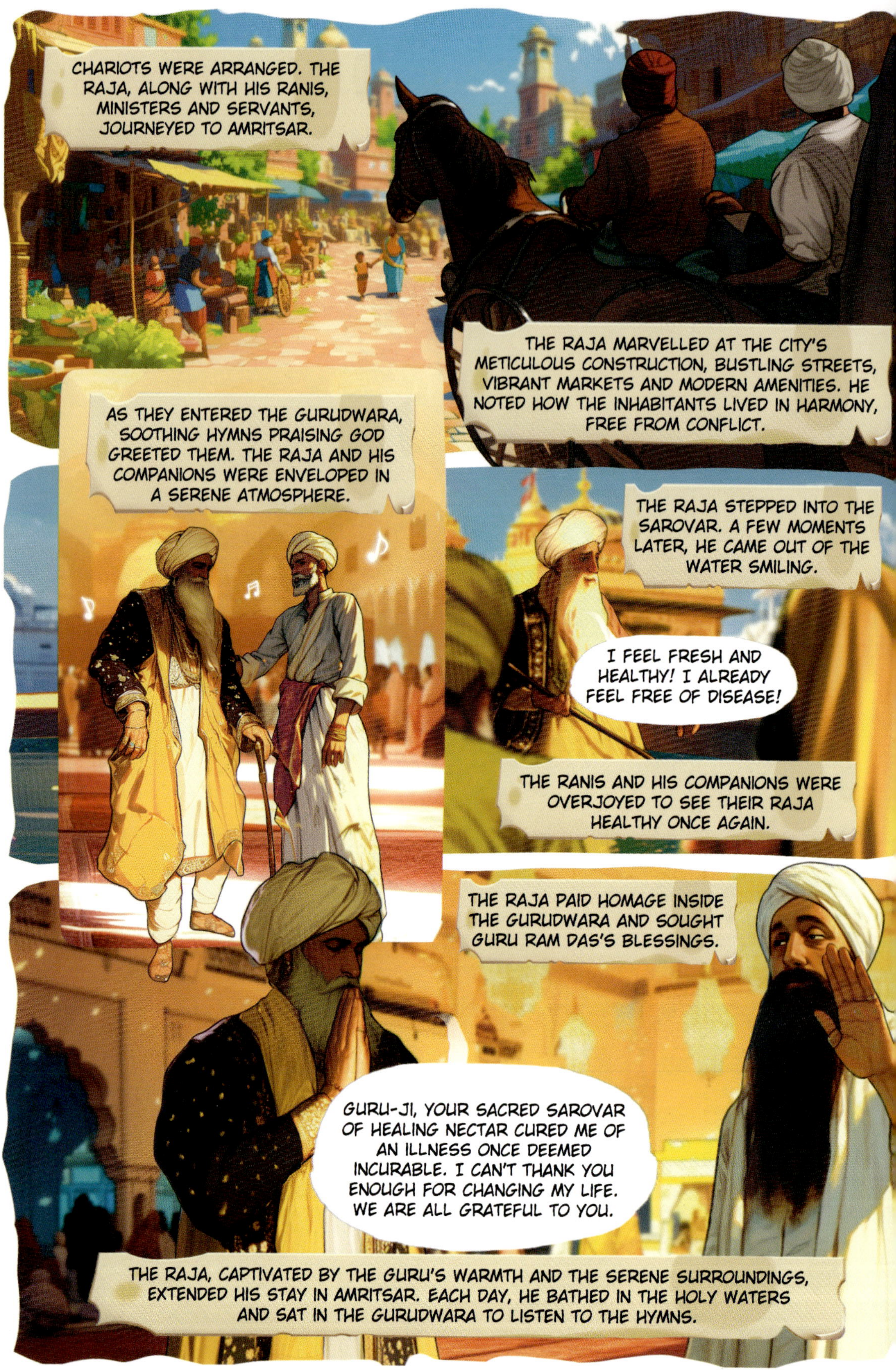
CHARIOTS WERE ARRANGED. THE RAJA, ALONG WITH HIS RANIS, MINISTERS AND SERVANTS, JOURNEYED TO AMRITSAR.
THE RAJA MARVELLED AT THE CITY'S METICULOUS CONSTRUCTION, BUSTLING STREETS, VIBRANT MARKETS AND MODERN AMENITIES. HE NOTED HOW THE INHABITANTS LIVED IN HARMONY, FREE FROM CONFLICT.
AS THEY ENTERED THE GURUDWARA, SOOTHING HYMNS PRAISING GOD GREETED THEM. THE RAJA AND HIS COMPANIONS WERE ENVELOPED IN A SERENE ATMOSPHERE.
THE RAJA STEPPED INTO THE SAROVAR. A FEW MOMENTS LATER, HE CAME OUT OF THE WATER SMILING.
I FEEL FRESH AND HEALTHY! I ALREADY FEEL FREE OF DISEASE!
THE RANIS AND HIS COMPANIONS WERE OVERJOYED TO SEE THEIR RAJA HEALTHY ONCE AGAIN.
THE RAJA PAID HOMAGE INSIDE THE GURUDWARA AND SOUGHT GURU RAM DAS'S BLESSINGS.
GURU-JI, YOUR SACRED SAROVAR OF HEALING NECTAR CURED ME OF AN ILLNESS ONCE DEEMED INCURABLE. I CAN'T THANK YOU ENOUGH FOR CHANGING MY LIFE. WE ARE ALL GRATEFUL TO YOU.
THE RAJA, CAPTIVATED BY THE GURU'S WARMTH AND THE SERENE SURROUNDINGS, EXTENDED HIS STAY IN AMRITSAR. EACH DAY, HE BATHED IN THE HOLY WATERS AND SAT IN THE GURUDWARA TO LISTEN TO THE HYMNS.

CAPTIVATED BY THE HEALING WORDS OF THESE HYMNS, THE RAJA BECAME A DEVOUT SIKH. NEWS OF HIS RECOVERY INSPIRED PEOPLE FROM MULTAN TO VISIT AMRITSAR TO MEET GURU RAM DAS AND TAKE A DIP IN THE HOLY WATERS. MANY CONVERTED TO SIKHISM AFTER EXPERIENCING THE TEACHINGS THERE.
ONCE, A BRAHMIN PRIEST REFUSED TO OFFICIATE THE WEDDING OF A YOUNG SIKH WOMAN BECAUSE HER FATHER COULDN'T AFFORD THE CEREMONIAL EXPENSES. TROUBLED, THE SIKH MAN TURNED TO GURU RAM DAS FOR HELP.
GURU RAM DAS INVITED THE BRIDE AND GROOM'S FAMILIES TO HIS COURT ON THE WEDDING DAY. HE RECITED A FOUR-STANZA HYMN, 'LAVAN', TO CONDUCT THE MARRIAGE WITH GREAT SIMPLICITY.
GURU RAM DAS DEFINED THE SIKH MARRIAGE WITH THESE WORDS: 'THEY ARE NOT HUSBAND AND WIFE WHO MERELY SIT TOGETHER. THEY ARE HUSBAND AND WIFE WHO HAVE ONE SOUL IN TWO BODIES.' THIS MARKED THE BEGINNING OF THE TRADITION OF RECITING LAVAN AT SIKH WEDDINGS, AND TO THIS DAY, IT REMAINS AN ESSENTIAL PART OF SIKH WEDDING CEREMONIES.
THE TEMPLE THAT GURU RAM DAS CONSTRUCTED, INSPIRED BY GURU AMAR DAS, CONTINUES TO BE ONE OF THE MOST IMPORTANT SITES FOR THE SIKH RELIGION. CALLED HARMANDIR SAHIB, WHICH MEANS 'A PLACE OF WORSHIP FOR ALL', IT REMAINS OPEN TO PEOPLE OF ALL FAITHS AND BACKGROUNDS.
GURU RAM DAS STRESSED THE IMPORTANCE OF SELFLESS SERVICE, BELIEVING THAT SERVING OTHERS WITHOUT EXPECTING A REWARD WAS A PATH TO SPIRITUAL GROWTH.
HE SERVED AS GURU FOR SEVEN YEARS UNTIL HIS PASSING ON 1 SEPTEMBER 1581.

# Guru Arjan Dev

(1563 - 1606)

*Teene Taap Nivaranhara, Dukh Hanta Sukh Raas*
*Tako Bighan Na Koun Lage, Ja Ki Prabh Aage Ardas*

God cures all pains, He gives us comforts.
He does not suffer any ills, if he prays with faith.

GURU ARJAN DEV, THE FIFTH GURU, WAS BORN ON 15 APRIL 1563, IN GOINDWAL. HE WAS ORIGINALLY NAMED ARJANMAL AND WAS THE YOUNGEST OF THREE SONS BORN TO GURU RAM DAS AND BIBI BHANI.
GURU ARJAN DEV BECAME GURU AT THE AGE OF EIGHTEEN.
HE WAS MARRIED TO GANGA, AND HAD A SON, HAR GOBIND, WHO LATER BECAME THE SIXTH GURU.
AFTER HIS FATHER'S DEATH, GURU ARJAN DEV CONTINUED THE CONSTRUCTION WORK OF THE SAROVAR AND GURUDWARA HARMANDIR SAHIB.
GURU-JI, LET'S BUILD THE GURUDWARA AS THE TALLEST BUILDING AROUND. THE TALLER IT IS, THE MORE RESPECT IT WILL GAIN.
I WANT THE HARMANDIR SAHIB TO BE THE LOWEST BUILDING, SYMBOLISING HUMILITY. ONE SHOULD STEP DOWN TO ENTER, REFLECTING SUBMISSION AND HUMILITY. AS MY FATHER ENVISIONED, THE GURUDWARA SHOULD HAVE DOORS ON ALL FOUR SIDES, WELCOMING EVERYONE FROM EVERY DIRECTION.
THE CONSTRUCTION WAS DONE WITH THE VOLUNTARY LABOUR OF HINDUS, MUSLIMS AND SIKHS FROM ACROSS INDIA. THEY OFFERED THEIR TAN (BODY), MANN (MIND) AND DHAN (EARNINGS) TO SEE TO THE COMPLETION OF THE TEMPLE.

AFTER THE CONSTRUCTION WAS COMPLETED, GURU ARJAN EXPRESSED HIS DESIRE TO RELOCATE FROM AMRITSAR DUE TO HIS BROTHER PRITHI CHAND'S PERSISTENT HOSTILITY. GURU ARJAN LEFT AMRITSAR WITH HIS FAMILY AND TOOK SHELTER IN A VILLAGE CALLED WADALI.
WHEN HIS SON, HAR GOBIND, TURNED TWO, SIKHS FROM AMRITSAR CAME TO VISIT THEIR GURU.
GURU-JI, PLEASE COME BACK TO AMRITSAR. MANY FOLLOWERS FROM DISTANT LANDS COME TO TAKE YOUR BLESSINGS, BUT THEY LEAVE DISAPPOINTED.
I WILL GO WITH YOU FIRST THING IN THE MORNING.
UPON REACHING AMRITSAR, GURU ARJAN WENT DIRECTLY TO HARMANDIR SAHIB.
EVERYONE, EXCEPT PRITHI CHAND, WAS HAPPY TO HAVE THEIR GURU BACK.
SO, HE IS BACK! I WILL WAIT FOR THE RIGHT TIME TO STRIKE.
MEANWHILE, GURU ARJAN BEGAN COMPILING GURU NANAK'S WRITINGS, OBTAINING THE ORIGINAL TEXTS FROM HIS UNCLE, MOHAN. WITH THE HELP OF HIS COMPANION, BHAI GURDAS, HE BEGAN WORKING ON THE COMPILATION OF THE HOLY BOOK, THE 'GURU GRANTH SAHIB'. HE INCLUDED THE WRITINGS OF OTHER SAINTS LIKE KABIR, BABA FARID AND RAVIDAS.

IE COMPOSED THE SUKHMANI SAHIB, AROUND THE YEAR 1602. HIS WORKS, POETIC REVELATIONS AND LETTERS ) HIS FATHER FROM LAHORE WERE INCLUDED IN THE ADI RANTH, THE FIRST VERSION F THE 'GURU GRANTH SAHIB'. 1604, THE ADI GRANTH WAS OMPLETED AND INSTALLED IN THE HARMANDIR SAHIB. THE RIGINAL ADI GRANTH, SIGNED BY GURU ARJAN, IS KEPT AT KARTARPUR.
AFTER INCORPORATING SCRIPTURES FROM ALL THE GURUS AND OTHER SAINTS, THE COLLECTION WAS FINALISED AS THE 'GURU GRANTH SAHIB.

A GROUP OF DEVOUT FOLLOWERS FROM KABUL TRAVELLED TO AMRITSAR. ALONG THE WAY, THEY MET A SIKH COUPLE. THROUGHOUT THE JOURNEY, THE COUPLE CARED FOR THE GROUP'S NEEDS, PROVIDING THEM WITH WATER, COOKING MEALS FOR THEM, FANNING THEM AND MASSAGING THEIR TIRED LEGS.

UPON ARRIVING IN MRITSAR THE NEXT DAY, THE TRAVELLERS FROM KABUL WAITED FOR ABOUT HALF AN HOUR AND COULDN'T FIND THE GURU.
WE CAME ALL THE WAY TO MEET GURU-JI. WHERE IS HE?
GURU-JI HAS GONE TO RECEIVE THE GROUP COMING FROM KABUL.
BUT WE ARE THE PEOPLE FROM KABUL!

DID GURU-JI NOT JOIN YOU ON THE WAY!?
NO! ONLY A SIKH COUPLE ACCOMPANIED US MIDWAY. THEY LOOKED AFTER US VERY WELL. WE LEFT THEM TO LOOK AFTER OUR SHOES.

THEY WENT IN SEARCH OF THE SIKH COUPLE AND FOUND THEM PLEASANTLY CLEANING THE SHOES OF THE TRAVELLERS.
GURU-JI, WE'VE BEEN LOOKING FOR YOU.
THE GROUP WAS STUNNED TO LEARN THAT THE PERSON WHO HAD BEEN CARING FOR THEM AND NOW CLEANING THEIR SHOES, WAS THE VERY GURU THEY CAME TO HONOUR. GURU ARJAN'S HUMILITY REINFORCED THE CORE SIKH PRINCIPLES OF SERVICE AND EQUALITY.
FROM 1581 TO 1606, SIKHISM FLOURISHED UNDER GURU ARJAN, ATTRACTING EVEN HINDU SAINTS AND MUSLIM PIRS. HOWEVER, HIS GROWING INFLUENCE AND SUPPORT FOR JEHANGIR'S REBELLIOUS SON, KHUSRAU, PROVOKED THE MUGHAL EMPEROR, LEADING TO FALSE ALLEGATIONS AGAINST THE GURU.
PRITHI CHAND FUELLED RUMOURS THAT LED TO GURU ARJAN FACING FALSE ACCUSATIONS OF INCLUDING ANTI-HINDU AND ANTI-MUSLIM CONTENT IN THE 'GURU GRANTH SAHIB'. HE DID THIS OUT OF HUMILIATION AND RESENTMENT OVER LOSING THE GURUSHIP TO GURU ARJAN.
CHANDU SHAH, A KHATRI FROM LAHORE WITH MUGHAL TIES, TURNED HOSTILE TOWARD GURU ARJAN AFTER HIS REJECTION OF A MARRIAGE PROPOSAL FOR HIS DAUGHTER. IN RESPONSE, CHANDU SHAH CONSPIRED WITH EMPEROR JEHANGIR AGAINST GURU ARJAN.

SPURRED BY THE DECEPTIONS OF CHANDU SHAH AND PRITHI CHAND, EMPEROR JEHANGIR SUMMONED GURU ARJAN TO HIS COURT IN LAHORE. HAZRAT MIAN MIR, A FAMOUS SUFI MUSLIM SAINT, PLEADED FOR GURU ARJAN.
I INTEND TO SENTENCE HIM TO DEATH. HE MUST FACE THE CONSEQUENCES.
YOUR HIGHNESS, PLEASE RECONSIDER. HE IS A MAN OF PEACE. PERHAPS REDUCE THE SENTENCE ON THE CONDITION THAT HE ERASES THOSE VERSES FROM THE 'GURU GRANTH SAHIB'.
KNOWING HE MIGHT NOT RETURN ALIVE DUE TO THE CHARGES AGAINST HIM, GURU ARJAN APPOINTED HIS SON, HAR GOBIND, AS THE NEXT GURU BEFORE HEADING TO THE MUGHAL COURT.
HEAR YOU'VE DISRESPECTED HINDU AND MUSLIM TRADITIONS IN YOUR HOLY BOOK. REMOVE THE OFFENSIVE SECTIONS, OR FACE EXECUTION.
I ONLY ADDRESSED THE RITUALS THAT ARE BEING FOLLOWED WITHOUT REASONING. I HAVE NOT DISRESPECTED ANY RELIGION.
HUH! IT IS YOUR WORD AGAINST MINE. AND TELL ME, WHY DID YOU SUPPORT MY SON, KHUSRAU, WHO HAD REBELLED AGAINST ME?
I INITIALLY REFUSED TO HELP YOUR SON BECAUSE I KNEW HE HAD REBELLED AGAINST YOU. BUT HE WAS STARVING AND ASKING FOR MONEY TO GET BACK ON HIS FEET. HOW COULD I REFUSE? I REGARD EVERYONE—HINDU, MUSLIM, RICH, POOR, FRIEND OR FOE—WITHOUT JUDGEMENT OR HATE.

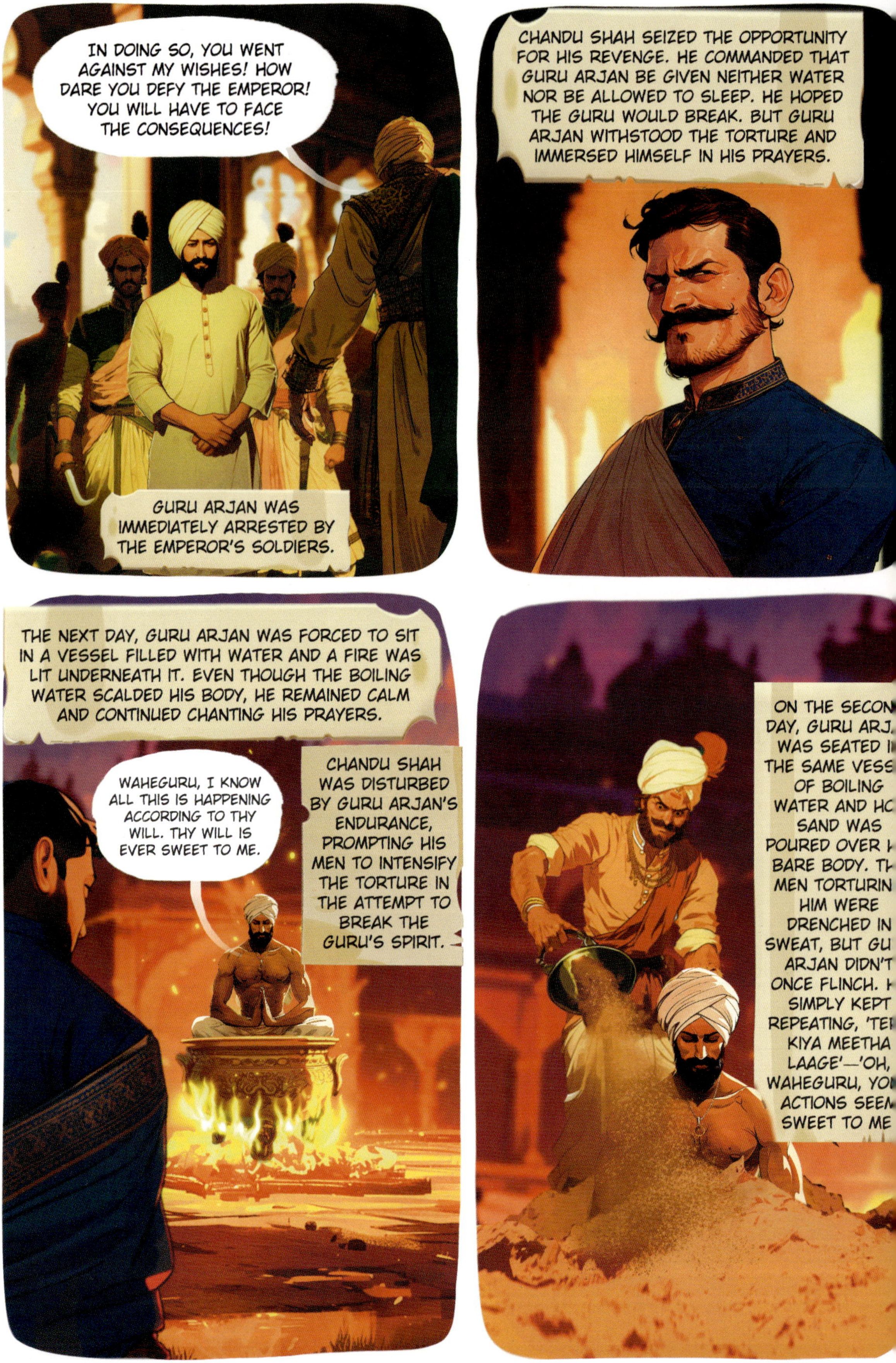
IN DOING SO, YOU WENT AGAINST MY WISHES! HOW DARE YOU DEFY THE EMPEROR! YOU WILL HAVE TO FACE THE CONSEQUENCES!
GURU ARJAN WAS IMMEDIATELY ARRESTED BY THE EMPEROR'S SOLDIERS.
CHANDU SHAH SEIZED THE OPPORTUNITY FOR HIS REVENGE. HE COMMANDED THAT GURU ARJAN BE GIVEN NEITHER WATER NOR BE ALLOWED TO SLEEP. HE HOPED THE GURU WOULD BREAK. BUT GURU ARJAN WITHSTOOD THE TORTURE AND IMMERSED HIMSELF IN HIS PRAYERS.
THE NEXT DAY, GURU ARJAN WAS FORCED TO SIT IN A VESSEL FILLED WITH WATER AND A FIRE WAS LIT UNDERNEATH IT. EVEN THOUGH THE BOILING WATER SCALDED HIS BODY, HE REMAINED CALM AND CONTINUED CHANTING HIS PRAYERS.
WAHEGURU, I KNOW ALL THIS IS HAPPENING ACCORDING TO THY WILL. THY WILL IS EVER SWEET TO ME.
CHANDU SHAH WAS DISTURBED BY GURU ARJAN'S ENDURANCE, PROMPTING HIS MEN TO INTENSIFY THE TORTURE IN THE ATTEMPT TO BREAK THE GURU'S SPIRIT.
ON THE SECON DAY, GURU ARJ WAS SEATED I THE SAME VESS OF BOILING WATER AND HO SAND WAS POURED OVER H BARE BODY. TH MEN TORTURIN HIM WERE DRENCHED IN SWEAT, BUT GU ARJAN DIDN'T ONCE FLINCH. H SIMPLY KEPT REPEATING, 'TE KIYA MEETHA LAAGE'—'OH, WAHEGURU, YO ACTIONS SEEM SWEET TO ME

THAT DAY, HAZRAT MIAN MIR VISITED THE GURU.
GURU-JI, I CANNOT BEAR TO SEE THESE ATROCITIES INFLICTED ON YOU.
EVERYTHING HAPPENING ALIGNS WITH WAHEGURU'S DIVINE WILL. THOSE WHO SPEAK THE TRUTH OFTEN FACE HARDSHIPS. PRAY FOR ME. PRAY FOR TRUTH TO PREVAIL.
NEXT DAY, GURU ARJAN WAS MADE TO SIT ON A HOT PLATE WHILE SCALDING SAND WAS POURED OVER HIS BODY.
TWO OF HIS DEVOTED FOLLOWERS, BHAI JAITHA AND BHAI PIRANA, WITNESSED THIS WHEN THEY CAME TO VISIT.
GURU-JI, IF ONLY WE COULD TAKE YOUR PLACE TO SPARE YOU THIS PAIN!
IT IS MY TIME TO LEAVE THIS WORLD. THERE IS A PURPOSE FOR MY SACRIFICE. YOU MUST ENSURE MY SACRIFICE DOES NOT GO IN VAIN.
ON THE FIFTH DAY, CHANDU SHAH PROPOSED COVERING GURU ARJAN WITH A FRESH COWHIDE AND THEN STITCHING THE HIDE AROUND HIM.
ONCE YOU'RE INSIDE THE COWHIDE AND PLACED IN THE SUN, THE DRYING HIDE WILL SQUEEZE AND CRUSH EVERY BONE IN YOUR BODY. YOU WILL REGRET REJECTING MY DAUGHTER'S HAND FOR YOUR SON!
I HAVE GONE WITHOUT FOOD, WATER OR SLEEP FOR FIVE DAYS. ALLOW ME TO BATHE IN THE RIVER FIRST.
CHANDU SHAH, BELIEVING THE COLD WATER WOULD ADD TO THE GURU'S SUFFERING, AGREED TO HIS REQUEST.

BY NOW, A HUGE CROWD OF PEOPLE HAD GATHERED AROUND.
WAHEGURU! WAHEGURU! YOU ARE THE GREATEST, GURU-JI! YOU ARE TRULY THE GREATEST MARTYR!
AS GURU ARJAN STEPPED INTO THE RAVI RIVER, HE MERGED WITH THE DIVINE LIGHT AND HIS PHYSICAL FORM VANISHED FROM SIGHT.

WHEN BHAI JAITHA AND BHAI PIRANA RETURNED TO AMRITSAR, THEY WENT TO THEIR GURU'S SON, HAR GOBIND.
OUR GURU HAS LEFT FOR HIS HEAVENLY HOME. YOU WILL BE OUR GURU NOW. IN HIS LAST MOMENTS, GURU-JI INSTRUCTED YOU TO RAISE AN ARMY AND FIGHT AGAINST THOSE WHO HAVE DONE EVIL.

IN 1606, GURU ARJAN DEV, THE FIRST SIKH GURU TO BE MARTYRED, SOWED THE SEED OF SACRIFICE AMONG THE SIKHS. THE GURUDWARA DERA SAHIB IN LAHORE, PAKISTAN, MARKS THE SITE WHERE GURU ARJAN WAS MARTYRED IN 1606, HONOURING HIS ULTIMATE SACRIFICE.

# Guru Har Gobind

(1595 - 1644)

*Achar Charre Taan Sidh Hoyee, Sidhee Te Budh Payee*

By eating the uneatable and tolerating that what is not tolerable
one obtains spiritual powers.
From controlling those powers, one obtains wisdom.

GURU HAR GOBIND WAS BORN IN WADALI, NEAR AMRITSAR, ON 19 JUNE 1595. AFTER BEING CHILDLESS FOR YEARS, MATA GANGA RECEIVED BLESSINGS FROM BABA BUDDHA AND ONLY AFTER THAT SHE WAS ABLE TO CONCEIVE.
HOWEVER, HAR GOBIND'S BIRTH SHATTERED THE HOPES OF PRITHI CHAND, WHO HAD WANTED HIS SON, MEHERBAN, TO BECOME THE NEXT GURU. PRITHI CHAND MADE MULTIPLE ATTEMPTS TO KILL HAR GOBIND, BUT HE FAILED EACH TIME.
GURU HAR GOBIND WAS JUST ELEVEN WHEN HIS FATHER, GURU ARJAN, THE FIFTH SIKH GURU, WAS MARTYRED IN LAHORE.
HE HONOURED HIS FATHER'S WISHES BY STANDING AGAINST THE OPPRESSIVE MUGHAL RULE. AS THE SIXTH GURU, HE LAID THE FOUNDATION FOR THE WARRIOR TRADITION IN SIKHISM.
AS GURU HAR GOBIND GREW OLDER, HE NOT ONLY DEEPENED HIS SPIRITUAL KNOWLEDGE BUT ALSO TRAINED IN HORSE RIDING, MARTIAL ARTS AND WARFARE. HE BECAME THE FIRST GURU TO WIELD WEAPONS AND EMPHASISE THE IMPORTANCE OF MARTIAL SKILLS FOR SELF-DEFENCE.
AT HIS SUCCESSION CEREMONY, INSTEAD OF WEARING THE 'SELI', A HEADGEAR REPRESENTING GURU NANAK'S LEGACY, HE ASKED BABA BUDDHA TO ADORN HIM WITH TWO SWORDS. HE NAMED THEM MIRI AND PIRI—TO REPRESENT HIS WORLDLY AND SPIRITUAL AUTHORITY, RESPECTIVELY.
HE ALSO STARTED WEARING A KALGI, A ROYAL ORNAMENT WORN ON THE TURBAN BY MUGHAL AND HINDU KINGS AND SAT ON A THRONE, AKIN TO OTHER KINGS. THESE GESTURES SIGNALLED HIS READINESS TO DEFEND SIKH RELIGION.

IN 1606, GURU HAR GOBIND ESTABLISHED THE AKAL TAKHAT, A 12-FOOT-HIGH PLATFORM IN FRONT OF THE HARMANDIR SAHIB. HE SAT THERE IN ROYAL ATTIRE, LISTENED TO HIS PEOPLE'S CONCERNS, AND ISSUED ORDERS AS A RULER WOULD.
THE HARMANDIR SAHIB REFLECTED GURU HAR GOBIND'S SPIRITUAL AUTHORITY, WHILE THE AKAL TAKHAT, THE FIRST HIGH PLATFORM IN SIKH HISTORY, SYMBOLISED HIS WORLDLY AUTHORITY.
HE BUILT THE LOHGARH FORT IN AMRITSAR, THE SIKHS' FIRST FORT, FOR DEFENCE OF THE CITY. HE ALSO ADOPTED THE SIKHS' FIRST FLAG. HIS FOLLOWERS BEGAN CALLING HIM 'SACHA PATSHAH', MEANING 'THE TRUE EMPEROR'.
THESE ROYAL WAR-LIKE ACTIVITIES OF GURU HAR GOBIND ANGERED HIS BITTER RIVALS, PRITHI CHAND AND CHANDU SHAH. THEY JOINED FORCES WITH LAHORE'S RULERS AND WENT TO MEET EMPEROR JEHANGIR.
JAHANPANAH, THE GURU SITS ON A THRONE! THRONES AREN'T FOR BEGGARS! HE'S BEEN CALLING HIMSELF 'THE TRUE KING' AND BUILDING AN ARMY. I BELIEVE HE'S SEEKING REVENGE FOR HIS FATHER'S DEATH.
I FEAR THE SAME, JAHANPANAH! YOU SHOULD SUMMON HIM AND REMIND HIM OF HIS PLACE BEFORE IT'S TOO LATE.
THE EMPEROR, FEARING THE SUDDEN SHIFT IN THE DIRECTION OF SIKHISM, SUMMONED GURU HAR GOBIND TO HIS COURT. BUT WHEN HE MET HIM, HE WAS STUNNED.
HE'S JUST A BOY. MAYBE I SHOULDN'T JUMP TO CONCLUSIONS AND CONSIDER HIM A THREAT.
THE EMPEROR QUESTIONED GURU HAR GOBIND ON SPIRITUAL MATTERS AND WAS IMPRESSED BY HIS WISDOM. GRADUALLY, HE WARMED UPTO THE YOUNG GURU. GURU HAR GOBIND KNEW THAT CHANDU SHAH WAS ACTUALLY THE ONE BEHIND HIS FATHER'S TORTURE. SO HE DIDN'T MIND CHOOSING THE EMPEROR'S OFFER OF FRIENDSHIP.

ONE DAY, HE AND THE EMPEROR WENT HORSEBACK RIDING IN THE JUNGLE. OUT OF NOWHERE, A TIGER SUDDENLY LEAPT IN FRONT, ATTACKING THE EMPEROR ON HIS HORSE.
SOMEONE, PLEASE SAVE THE JAHANPANAH!
GURU HAR GOBIND QUICKLY STEPPED IN-BETWEEN THE EMPEROR AND THE TIGER. HE DREW HIS SWORD AND KILLED THE BEAST.
HE RISKED HIS LIFE FOR ME! IF HE WAS OUT TO AVENGE HIS FATHER, HE COULD'VE EASILY LET ME DIE. I'M GLAD I DID NOT GET INFLUENCED BY MY ADVISORS.
AS THEIR FRIENDSHIP GREW, CHANDU SHAH STARTED FEARING RETRIBUTION FOR THE LATE GURU ARJAN'S DEATH. SO, WHEN THE EMPEROR FELL SERIOUSLY ILL, AND THERE WAS NO CURE IN SIGHT, CHANDU SHAH SAW HIS CHANCE. HE BRIBED THE COURT ASTROLOGER TO SPEAK WITH THE EMPEROR.
JAHANPANAH, YOUR ILLNESS IS NOT DUE TO A DISEASE. IT IS CAUSED BY UNFAVOURABLE STARS. ALL YOUR STARS ARE IN RETROGRADE, WHICH COULD BRING SEVEN YEARS OF MISFORTUNE. THERE'S A REMEDY, BUT ...
BUT WHAT? TELL ME RIGHT NOW! YOU HAVE PUT MY MIND AT DEEP UNREST.
YOUR COSMIC CHART SUGGEST THAT IF SOMEONE NAMED HAR GOBIND PRAYS FOR YOU FOR FOR DAYS, THE ALIGNMENT OF YOUR STARS COULD IMPROVE. HOWEVE HE MUST STAY IN A REMOTE LOCATION, PERFORMING RITUAL BATHS AND DEVOTIONAL PRACTIC DAILY, UNTIL WE SEE A CHANGE
I THINK THE GWALIOR FORT WOULD BE AN IDEAL PLACE FOR THIS.
THE ASTROLOGER AND CHANDU SHAH KEPT PUSHING THE IDEA. DESPITE HIS RELUCTANCE, EMPEROR JEHANGIR EVENTUALLY AGREED.

HE EMPEROR, WITH A HEAVY HEART, MET GURU HAR GOBIND TO SHARE HIS ASTROLOGER'S ADVICE. THE GURU INSTANTLY RECOGNISED THE MANIPULATION AT PLAY BUT CHOSE NOT TO REVEAL IT TO THE EMPEROR.
IF IT EASES YOUR MIND, I WILL GO TO GWALIOR.
OH, YOU ARE THE TRUE GURU. I KNOW YOU WILL PROTECT ME FROM MISFORTUNE.
GURU HAR GOBIND WAS TAKEN TO THE GWALIOR ORT. BUT THE FORT WAS MORE LIKE A PRISON. ALL THOSE WHO EMPEROR JEHANGIR FELT THREATENED BY WERE BROUGHT THERE AND IMPRISONED FOR LIFE.
AMONG THE PRISONERS WERE FIFTY-TWO KINGS. THEY WERE SHACKLED AND LOOKED MALNOURISHED. WHEN THEY SAW GURU HAR GOBIND, THEY SMILED FOR THE FIRST TIME IN A VERY LONG WHILE.
WE USED TO BE ROYALTY, BUT NOW WE LIVE LIKE RATS! BUT SEEING YOU GIVES US HOPE.
WE ARE BLESSED TO HAVE YOUR 'DARSHAN'. GREAT IS THE GURU!
WHEN GURU HAR GOBIND'S MOTHER, MATA GANGA, HEARD THE NEWS, SHE WAS EXTREMELY DISTURBED. THE SIKHS FEARED HAT THEIR GURU VOULD MEET THE SAME FATE AS HIS FATHER.
DO EVERYTHING IN YOUR POWER TO ENSURE MY SON'S PROMPT RETURN TO AMRITSAR!

THE SIKHS GATHERED TOGETHER IN LARGE NUMBERS OUTSIDE THE GWALIOR FORT AND BOWED BEFORE THE WALLS BEHIND WHICH THEIR GURU WAS CONFINED.
THEIR PRESENCE MADE THE EMPEROR UNEASY, BUT HE WAS STILL UNWELL, SO HE DIDN'T TAKE ANY ACTION.
THOUGH GURU HAR GOBIND WAS SUPPOSED TO BE CONFINED FOR FORTY DAYS, EIGHTEEN MONTHS PASSED WITHOUT HIS RELEASE. WAZIR KHAN, THE EMPEROR'S COUNCILLOR AND HAZRAT MIAN MIR, A SUFI SAINT, DECIDED TO APPEAL TO THE EMPEROR.
JAHANPANAH, YOU'VE BEEN HEALTHY FOR QUITE SOME TIME. I REQUEST THAT YOU RELEASE GURU-JI. HE DOES NOT POSE A THREAT TO YOUR THRONE.
GURU-JI HAS STAYED IN CONFINEMENT ONLY BECAUSE YOU ASKED HIM TO. HE COULD HAVE USED HIS SPIRITUAL POWERS TO ESCAPE, BUT HE RESPECTS YOU. PLEASE RELEASE HIM.
YOU'RE RIGHT. I ORDER THE GURU'S IMMEDIATE RELEASE!
WAZIR KHAN INFORMED THE EMPEROR ABOUT GURU'S CONDITION FOR HIS RELEASE: HE WANTED THE FIFTY-TWO IMPRISONED KINGS TO BE FREED AS WELL. THE EMPEROR, FEARING THEY MIGHT REBEL AGAIN IF RELEASED, PROPOSED A COMPROMISE.
TELL THE GURU THAT ALL THE KINGS WHO CAN HOLD ON TO HIS CLOTHING WHEN HE WALKS OUT OF THE FORT, WILL BE RELEASED.
ON HEARING THE EMPEROR'S PROPOSAL, GURU HAR GOBIND ORDERED HIS TAILOR TO MAKE HIM A LONG SASH TO TIE AROUND HIS WAIST, THAT WOULD TRAIL BEHIND HIM FOR MILES.
WHEN THE GATES OF THE PRISON WERE THROWN OPEN, ALL FIFTY-TWO KINGS, CLUTCHING ONTO THE SASH, WALKED OUT TO EMBRACE THEIR FREEDOM.

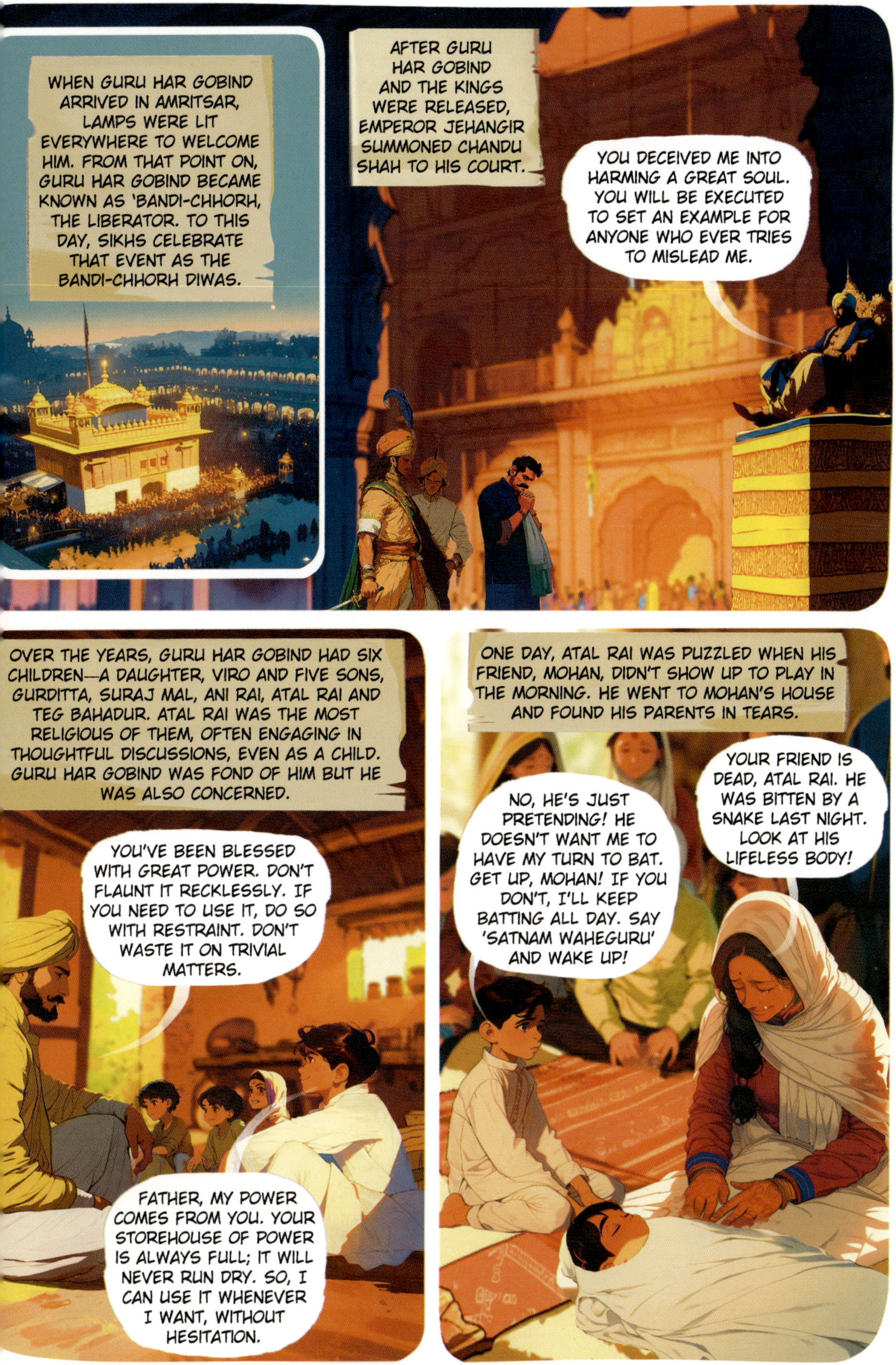
WHEN GURU HAR GOBIND ARRIVED IN AMRITSAR, LAMPS WERE LIT EVERYWHERE TO WELCOME HIM. FROM THAT POINT ON, GURU HAR GOBIND BECAME KNOWN AS 'BANDI-CHHORH, THE LIBERATOR. TO THIS DAY, SIKHS CELEBRATE THAT EVENT AS THE BANDI-CHHORH DIWAS.
AFTER GURU HAR GOBIND AND THE KINGS WERE RELEASED, EMPEROR JEHANGIR SUMMONED CHANDU SHAH TO HIS COURT.
YOU DECEIVED ME INTO HARMING A GREAT SOUL. YOU WILL BE EXECUTED TO SET AN EXAMPLE FOR ANYONE WHO EVER TRIES TO MISLEAD ME.
OVER THE YEARS, GURU HAR GOBIND HAD SIX CHILDREN—A DAUGHTER, VIRO AND FIVE SONS, GURDITTA, SURAJ MAL, ANI RAI, ATAL RAI AND TEG BAHADUR. ATAL RAI WAS THE MOST RELIGIOUS OF THEM, OFTEN ENGAGING IN THOUGHTFUL DISCUSSIONS, EVEN AS A CHILD. GURU HAR GOBIND WAS FOND OF HIM BUT HE WAS ALSO CONCERNED.
YOU'VE BEEN BLESSED WITH GREAT POWER. DON'T FLAUNT IT RECKLESSLY. IF YOU NEED TO USE IT, DO SO WITH RESTRAINT. DON'T WASTE IT ON TRIVIAL MATTERS.
FATHER, MY POWER COMES FROM YOU. YOUR STOREHOUSE OF POWER IS ALWAYS FULL; IT WILL NEVER RUN DRY. SO, I CAN USE IT WHENEVER I WANT, WITHOUT HESITATION.
ONE DAY, ATAL RAI WAS PUZZLED WHEN HIS FRIEND, MOHAN, DIDN'T SHOW UP TO PLAY IN THE MORNING. HE WENT TO MOHAN'S HOUSE AND FOUND HIS PARENTS IN TEARS.
NO, HE'S JUST PRETENDING! HE DOESN'T WANT ME TO HAVE MY TURN TO BAT. GET UP, MOHAN! IF YOU DON'T, I'LL KEEP BATTING ALL DAY. SAY 'SATNAM WAHEGURU' AND WAKE UP!
YOUR FRIEND IS DEAD, ATAL RAI. HE WAS BITTEN BY A SNAKE LAST NIGHT. LOOK AT HIS LIFELESS BODY!

SUDDENLY, THE WHITE SHEET SLID OFF AND MOHAN SAT UP, YAWNING AS IF WAKING UP FROM DEEP SLEEP.
THERE WERE CRIES OF WONDER ALL AROUND. THE MIRACLE CAUSED QUITE A STIR IN THE WHOLE VILLAGE. NEWS BEGAN SPREADING FAST, BEYOND THE VILLAGE TOO.
GURU HAR GOBIND WAS TROUBLED BY THE NEWS AND SUMMONED ATAL RAI.
YOU'VE MISUSED YOUR POWERS! NOW, PEOPLE WILL EXPECT US TO BRING THE DEAD BACK TO LIFE. WE CAN'T INTERFERE WITH GOD'S PLAN. YOUR GRANDFATHER, GURU ARJAN DEV, SET AN EXAMPLE OF ENDURANCE BY EMBRACING MARTYRDOM DESPITE HAVING SUCH POWERS.
I BROUGHT BACK A LIFE. I UNDERSTAND I NOW OWE A LIFE IN RETURN.
SAYING THAT, ATAL RAI WENT TO BATHE IN THE SAROVAR. HE UTTERED THE WORDS 'SATNAM WAHEGURU' AND WITH THOSE WORDS, HE DEPARTED FROM THE WORLD.
WHEN GURU HAR GOBIND RECEIVED THE NEWS OF HIS SON'S PASSING, HE WAS GREATLY UPSET. YET, HE ADVISED HIS FAMILY AND EVERYONE ELSE NOT TO GRIEVE.
ALL THOSE BORN MUST EVENTUALLY DEPART, SUCH IS THE WILL OF GOD.

GURU HAR GOBIND USED TO TRAVEL TO JAMMU AND KASHMIR, GUJARAT AND VARIOUS OTHER PLACES TO PREACH AND SPREAD THE MESSAGE OF SIKHISM. HE GARNERED NUMEROUS FOLLOWERS ALONG THE WAY.
IN 1628, SHAH JAHAN ASCENDED THE MUGHAL THRONE AFTER HAVING EXECUTED HIS KIN AND DESTROYED TEMPLES IN LAHORE. HE EVEN DESECRATED GURU ARJAN'S BAOLI AND CONVERTED THE LANGAR HALL INTO A MOSQUE, SPARKING CLASHES. GURU HAR GOBIND WON FOUR BATTLES, DIRECTLY CHALLENGING THE MUGHAL GENERALS IN ORDER TO MINIMISE CIVILIAN CASUALTIES. STILL MANY LIVES WERE LOST AS NO MUGHAL GENERAL DARED FACE HIM ALONE.
TO PREVENT FURTHER VIOLENCE, GURU HAR GOBIND RELOCATED TO KIRATPUR, A SMALL VILLAGE IN THE HIMALAYAN FOOTHILLS, FAR FROM MUSLIM ADMINISTRATIVE CENTRES LIKE LAHORE AND SIRHIND. HE SPENT THE LAST NINE YEARS OF HIS LIFE THERE, FOCUSING ON TEACHING AND SPREADING GURU NANAK'S MESSAGE.
IN 1644, GURU HAR GOBIND NAMED HIS FOURTEEN-YEAR-OLD GRANDSON, HAR RAI, AS THE NEXT GURU, BYPASSING HIS TWO SONS AND HIS ELDER GRANDSON, DHIR MAL, DEEMING THEM UNSUITABLE FOR THE ROLE.
THAT EVENING, AT THE AGE OF FORTY-NINE, GURU HAR GOBIND PASSED AWAY.
AFTER HIM, NONE OF THE GURUS EVER LIVED IN AMRITSAR.

# Guru Har Rai

(1630 - 1661)

*Sabhna Man Maanik Thaahan Mool Machaangava*
*Je Tau Pireeya Dhee Sik Hiaau Na Thaahe Kahi Da*

Every heart is a jewel, it's not good to break it.
If you long to see the Beloved Lord, never hurt anyone's feelings.

GURU HAR RAI, REVERED AS THE COMPASSIONATE GURU, WAS BORN IN 1630 IN KARTARPUR, IN PRESENT-DAY PAKISTAN. AT THE YOUNG AGE OF SEVEN, HE WAS MARRIED TO KISHAN KAUR. THEY LATER HAD TWO SONS, BABA RAM RAI AND SRI HAR KRISHAN.
FROM A VERY YOUNG AGE, GURU HAR RAI DEMONSTRATED A PROFOUND UNDERSTANDING OF THE 'GURU GRANTH SAHIB' AND SIKH HISTORY. HE WAS ALSO KNOWN FOR HIS ENVIRONMENTAL AWARENESS. HE ESTABLISHED THE GURU KA BAGH, AT KIRATPUR, WHERE HE GREW MEDICINAL PLANTS, FRUIT TREES AND RARE HERBS.
HE SET UP HOSPITALS AND USED THE HERBS FROM HIS GARDEN TO HEAL THOSE IN NEED. MARCH 14, THE DAY HE BECAME GURU, IS NOW CELEBRATED AS SIKH ENVIRONMENT DAY.
FOLLOWING THE TEACHINGS OF HIS GRANDFATHER AND FATHER, GURU HAR RAI EMPHASISED NON-VIOLENCE EVEN DURING TURBULENT TIMES. THOUGH HE WAS A MAN OF PEACE, HE MAINTAINED THE SIKH ARMY ESTABLISHED BY HIS GRANDFATHER, GURU HAR GOBIND.
DURING EMPEROR SHAH JAHAN'S REIGN, AMIDST SEVERE DROUGHT AND FAMINE IN INDIA, GURU HAR RAI ESTABLISHED LANGARS TO ENSURE NO ONE WENT HUNGRY. HE OPENED SHELTERS FOR LEPERS AND PROVIDED TREATMENT WITH MEDICINAL HERBS.

DARA SHIKOH, SHAH JAHAN'S ELDEST SON AND HEIR TO THE THRONE, WAS POISONED BY HIS AMBITIOUS BROTHER, AURANGZEB. UNAWARE OF THE TREACHERY, DARA SHIKOH HAD CONSUMED FOOD LACED WITH TIGER'S WHISKERS AND FELL GRAVELY ILL.
PHYSICIANS FROM ALL OVER THE COUNTRY COULDN'T HEAL HIM. THEY NEEDED A SPECIFIC HERB THAT WAS NOWHERE TO BE FOUND.
I HEAR THAT THE HERB WE SEEK IS ONLY AVAILABLE IN GURU HAR RAI'S DISPENSARY.
THE EMPEROR SHAH JAHAN WROTE A HUMBLE LETTER TO GURU HAR RAI, WHO IMMEDIATELY SENT THE MEDICINAL HERB THAT HEALED DARA SHIKOH.
FROM THAT MOMENT, EMPEROR SHAH JAHAN VOWED NEVER TO HARM THE GURU OR HIS PURPOSE.
GURU-JI, WHY DID YOU HELP THE EMPEROR, WHO HAS BEEN SO CRUEL TO YOUR FATHER AND GRANDFATHER?
THE AXE CUTS THE SANDAL TREE, YET THE SANDAL PERFUMES THE AXE. SIMILARLY, BY ADDRESSING EVIL WITH GOODNESS, THE GOOD WILL ENVELOP THE EVIL, TRANSFORMING IT WITH ITS OWN QUALITIES.
THIS INCIDENT EXEMPLIFIED GURU HAR RAI'S PHILOSOPHY OF NON-VIOLENCE, WHICH HE UPHELD THROUGHOUT HIS LIFE.

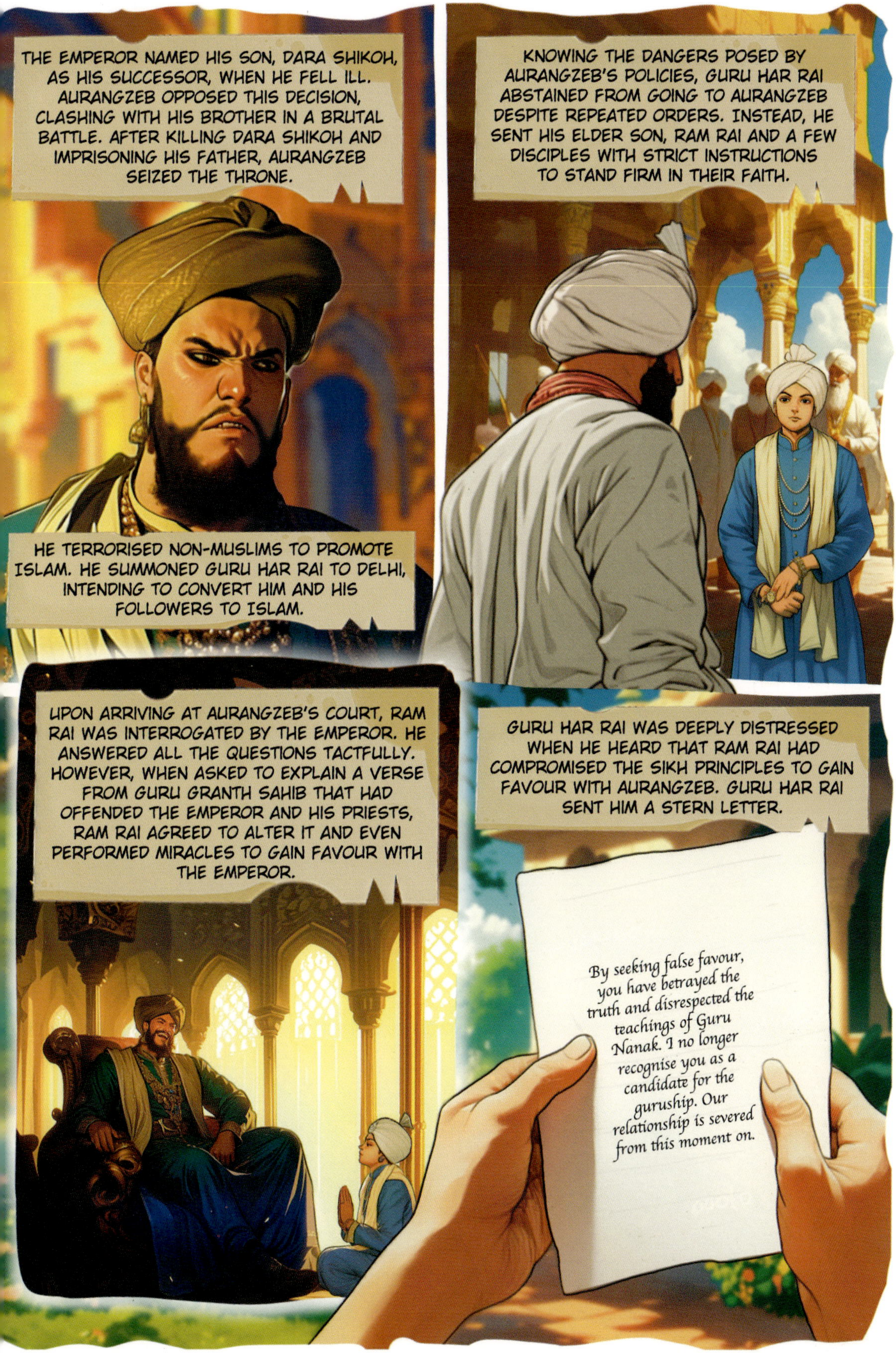
THE EMPEROR NAMED HIS SON, DARA SHIKOH, AS HIS SUCCESSOR, WHEN HE FELL ILL. AURANGZEB OPPOSED THIS DECISION, CLASHING WITH HIS BROTHER IN A BRUTAL BATTLE. AFTER KILLING DARA SHIKOH AND IMPRISONING HIS FATHER, AURANGZEB SEIZED THE THRONE.
HE TERRORISED NON-MUSLIMS TO PROMOTE ISLAM. HE SUMMONED GURU HAR RAI TO DELHI, INTENDING TO CONVERT HIM AND HIS FOLLOWERS TO ISLAM.
KNOWING THE DANGERS POSED BY AURANGZEB'S POLICIES, GURU HAR RAI ABSTAINED FROM GOING TO AURANGZEB DESPITE REPEATED ORDERS. INSTEAD, HE SENT HIS ELDER SON, RAM RAI AND A FEW DISCIPLES WITH STRICT INSTRUCTIONS TO STAND FIRM IN THEIR FAITH.
UPON ARRIVING AT AURANGZEB'S COURT, RAM RAI WAS INTERROGATED BY THE EMPEROR. HE ANSWERED ALL THE QUESTIONS TACTFULLY. HOWEVER, WHEN ASKED TO EXPLAIN A VERSE FROM GURU GRANTH SAHIB THAT HAD OFFENDED THE EMPEROR AND HIS PRIESTS, RAM RAI AGREED TO ALTER IT AND EVEN PERFORMED MIRACLES TO GAIN FAVOUR WITH THE EMPEROR.
GURU HAR RAI WAS DEEPLY DISTRESSED WHEN HE HEARD THAT RAM RAI HAD COMPROMISED THE SIKH PRINCIPLES TO GAIN FAVOUR WITH AURANGZEB. GURU HAR RAI SENT HIM A STERN LETTER.
By seeking false favour, you have betrayed the truth and disrespected the teachings of Guru Nanak. I no longer recognise you as a candidate for the guruship. Our relationship is severed from this moment on.

GURU HAR RAI BOLSTERED SIKHISM BY SENDING MISSIONARIES ACROSS THE COUNTRY TO SPREAD GURU NANAK'S MESSAGE. HIS COMMITMENT TO SOCIAL WELFARE AND FOSTERING INTERFAITH HARMONY WAS EVIDENT IN HIS ENDEAVOURS.
AS HIS LIFE NEARED ITS END, GURU HAR RAI DESIGNATED HIS FIVE-YEAR-OLD SON, HAR KRISHAN, AS HIS SUCCESSOR.
FINALLY, GURU HAR RAI, WHO GUIDED THE SIKH COMMUNITY FOR NINETEEN YEARS, PASSED AWAY IN 1661, AT THE AGE OF THIRTY-ONE.
GURU HAR RAI'S LIFE EXEMPLIFIED HOW COMPASSION CAN ILLUMINATE EVEN THE DARKEST OF TIMES. HIS LEGACY ENDURES, IMPARTING THE LESSON TO HIS FOLLOWERS TO EXTEND KINDNESS TO ALL, AS IT IS THE PATH TO TRUE ENLIGHTENMENT.

# Guru Har Krishan

(1656 - 1664)

*Sri Har Krishan Dhiyaye, Jis Dithe Sab Dukh Jaye*

The mere sight of Guru Sri Har Krishan dispels all sorrow.

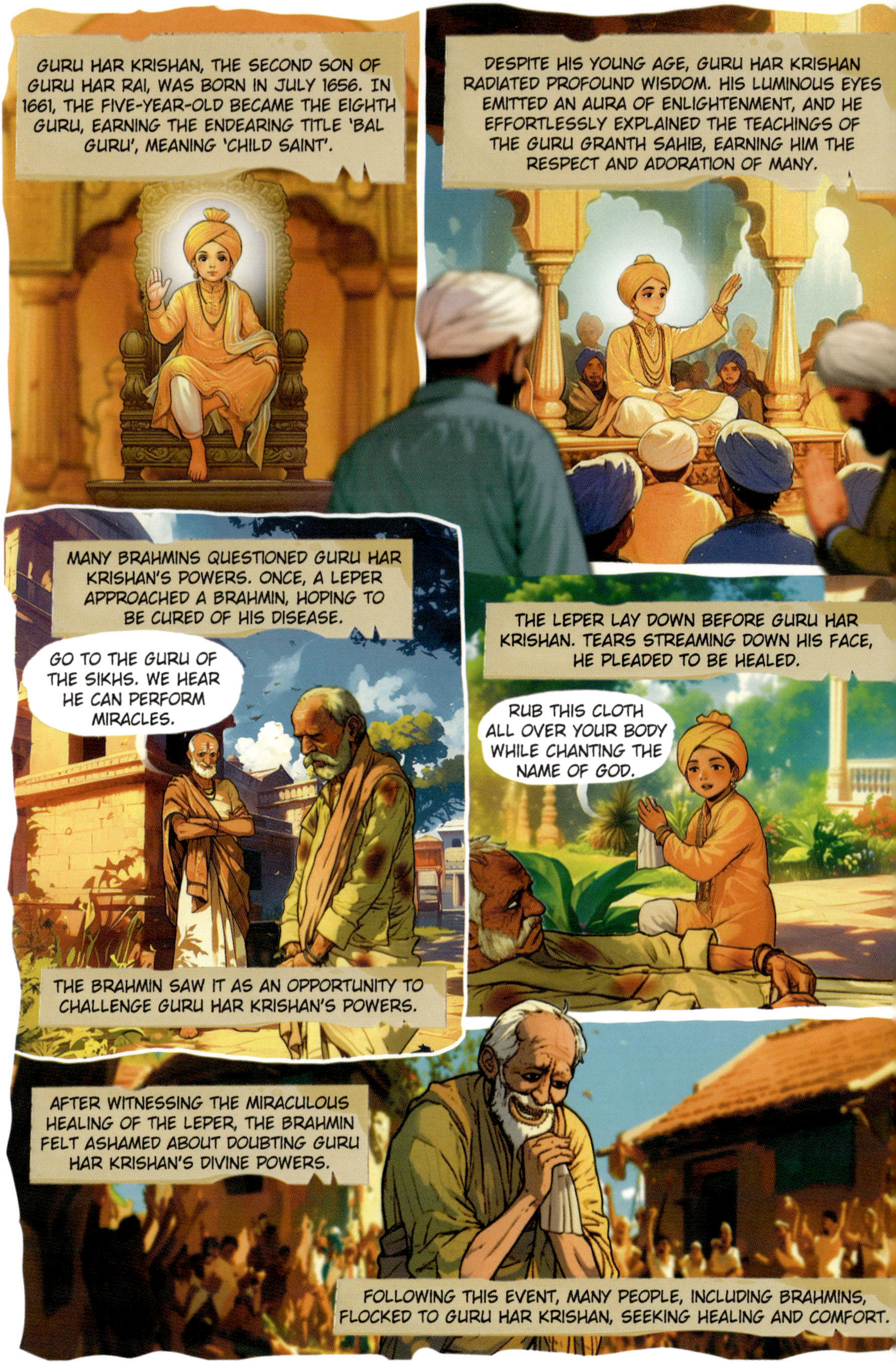

GURU HAR KRISHAN, THE SECOND SON OF GURU HAR RAI, WAS BORN IN JULY 1656. IN 1661, THE FIVE-YEAR-OLD BECAME THE EIGHTH GURU, EARNING THE ENDEARING TITLE 'BAL GURU', MEANING 'CHILD SAINT'.
DESPITE HIS YOUNG AGE, GURU HAR KRISHAN RADIATED PROFOUND WISDOM. HIS LUMINOUS EYES EMITTED AN AURA OF ENLIGHTENMENT, AND HE EFFORTLESSLY EXPLAINED THE TEACHINGS OF THE GURU GRANTH SAHIB, EARNING HIM THE RESPECT AND ADORATION OF MANY.
MANY BRAHMINS QUESTIONED GURU HAR KRISHAN'S POWERS. ONCE, A LEPER APPROACHED A BRAHMIN, HOPING TO BE CURED OF HIS DISEASE.
GO TO THE GURU OF THE SIKHS. WE HEAR HE CAN PERFORM MIRACLES.
THE BRAHMIN SAW IT AS AN OPPORTUNITY TO CHALLENGE GURU HAR KRISHAN'S POWERS.
THE LEPER LAY DOWN BEFORE GURU HAR KRISHAN. TEARS STREAMING DOWN HIS FACE, HE PLEADED TO BE HEALED.
RUB THIS CLOTH ALL OVER YOUR BODY WHILE CHANTING THE NAME OF GOD.
AFTER WITNESSING THE MIRACULOUS HEALING OF THE LEPER, THE BRAHMIN FELT ASHAMED ABOUT DOUBTING GURU HAR KRISHAN'S DIVINE POWERS.
FOLLOWING THIS EVENT, MANY PEOPLE, INCLUDING BRAHMINS, FLOCKED TO GURU HAR KRISHAN, SEEKING HEALING AND COMFORT.

RAM RAI, GURU HAR KRISHAN'S ELDER BROTHER, WAS RESENTFUL AFTER BEING DISOWNED BY THEIR FATHER. SEEKING REVENGE, HE APPROACHED THE MUGHAL EMPEROR AURANGZEB FOR HIS SUPPORT. INFLUENCED BY RAM RAI'S NARRATIVE, AURANGZEB SCHEMED TO MEET GURU HAR KRISHAN.
HE INTENDED TO ENCOURAGE HOSTILITY BETWEEN THE BROTHERS TO WEAKEN THEIR INFLUENCE OVER THE SIKH COMMUNITY. AURANGZEB'S PLAN WAS TO MAKE IT EASIER FOR SIKHS TO CONVERT TO ISLAM, THEREBY WEAKENING SIKH RESISTANCE.
THE EMPEROR CALLED FOR RAJA JAI SINGH, HIS SENIOR COURT OFFICIAL.
I WISH TO SEE THE GURU. PLEASE INVITE HIM TO MY COURT.
RAJA JAI SINGH WAS KNOWN FOR HIS DEVOTION TO THE SIKH GURUS. HE SENT A HIGH-RANKING OFFICIAL TO INVITE GURU HAR KRISHAN AND RESPECTFULLY ESCORT HIM TO DELHI.
MY FATHER ADVISED ME AGAINST MEETING EMPEROR AURANGZEB BECAUSE HE LED MY BROTHER ASTRAY. HENCE, I MUST RESPECTFULLY DECLINE THE INVITATION.
THE OFFICIAL DELIVERED GURU HAR KRISHAN'S MESSAGE TO RAJA JAI SINGH, WHO REALISED HE MUST EXTEND A PERSONAL INVITATION TO THE GURU.
The Sikhs in Delhi are eager to meet their revered Guru. You shall be my honoured guest while you are here. It is entirely up to you whether you wish to meet the emperor or not.
TOUCHED BY THIS COURTEOUS INVITATION, GURU HAR KRISHAN HEADED TO DELHI THE FOLLOWING DAY.
IN DELHI, GURU HAR KRISHAN RECEIVED A WARM WELCOME FROM THE SIKH COMMUNITY. AWARE OF THE GURU'S RELUCTANCE TO MEET HIM, THE EMPEROR SENT JEWELS, FINE CLOTHES AND A ROSARY TO ENTICE HIM. GURU HAR KRISHAN ACCEPTED ONLY THE ROSARY AND RETURNED THE REST, INDICATING HIS DISINTEREST IN WORLDLY RICHES.

WHILE HE WAS IMPRESSED BY GURU HAR KRISHAN'S REJECTION OF THE BRIBE, THE EMPEROR REMAINED INTENT ON TESTING THE GURU'S HOLINESS. HE DEVISED A PLAN AND ASKED RAJA JAI SINGH TO DISGUISE HIS WIFE AS A MAID AND DRESS ALL THE QUEEN'S HELPERS IN ROYAL ATTIRE FOLLOWING THIS PLAN, RAJA JAI SINGH SUMMONED GURU HAR KRISHAN TO THE COURT.
AS GURU HAR KRISHAN ENTERED, HE WAS GREETED BY THE ELEGANTLY DRESSED WOMEN. YET, HE WENT STRAIGHT TO THE ONE WHO WAS MODESTLY ATTIRED.
WHY IS THE RANI DRESSED AS A MAID?
THE QUEEN WAS ASTONISHED THAT THE GURU HAD RECOGNISED HER, DESPITE HER DISGUISE. REMORSEFUL, SHE BOWED HER HEAD IN RESPECT.
RAJA JAI SINGH INFORMED THE EMPEROR THAT THE PRANK ON GURU HAR KRISHAN HAD FAILED.
I ACKNOWLEDGE THAT GURU HAR KRISHAN IS A SAINT WITH POWERS. HE TRULY IS THE GURU THAT HIS FOLLOWERS CLAIM HIM TO BE.
AURANGZEB BECAME INCREASINGLY EAGER TO MEET GURU HAR KRISHAN. ONE DAY, HE LEFT HIS PALACE IN SECRET AND WENT ALONE TO RAJA JAI SINGH'S HOUSE, WHERE THE GURU WAS STAYING.
CLOSE THE DOOR AND LET THE EMPEROR KNOW THAT I WILL NEVER GIVE HIM AN AUDIENCE.
THE EMPEROR HAD TO RETURN DISAPPOINTED.

GURU HAR KRISHAN'S ARRIVAL IN DELHI QUICKLY DREW ATTENTION. WITH HIS WARMTH AND HIS ABILITY TO TOUCH PEOPLE'S LIVES, HIS FOLLOWERS INCREASED. RAJA JAI SINGH'S RESIDENCE BECAME A SPIRITUAL HUB AND CAME TO BE KNOWN AS GURUDWARA BANGLA SAHIB.
WHILE HE WAS IN DELHI, A SMALLPOX EPIDEMIC BROKE OUT IN THE CITY. SEVEN-YEAR-OLD GURU HAR KRISHAN DISPLAYED EXTRAORDINARY COMPASSION, PERSONALLY CARING FOR THE AFFLICTED, REGARDLESS OF THEIR CASTE. HE BLESSED A NEARBY LAKE'S WATER, WHICH REPORTEDLY HELPED THOUSANDS RECOVER.
GRATEFUL FOR HIS SELFLESS SERVICE, THE LOCAL MUSLIM COMMUNITY BEGAN CALLING HIM 'BALA PIR'. UNFORTUNATELY, WHILE TENDING TO THE SICK, GURU HAR KRISHAN CONTRACTED SMALLPOX AND HIS YOUNG BODY SOON SUCCUMBED TO THE DISEASE.
BEFORE TAKING HIS LAST BREATH, GURU HAR KRISHAN WAS ASKED TO NAME HIS SUCCESSOR. HE WHISPERED THE WORDS, 'BABA BAKALA', INDICATING THAT THE NEXT GURU WOULD BE DISCOVERED IN THE VILLAGE OF BAKALA, NEAR AMRITSAR.
HIS ALLUSION WAS TO TEGH BAHADUR, HIS GRANDFATHER'S BROTHER, WHO WAS RESIDING IN BAKALA AT THE TIME.
GURU HAR KRISHAN'S LIFE EXEMPLIFIES THAT SPIRITUALITY TRANSCENDS AGE AND FLOWS FROM A PURE AND ENLIGHTENED HEART. HIS SELFLESSNESS, ESPECIALLY DURING THE SMALLPOX EPIDEMIC, EPITOMISES THE SIKH PRINCIPLE OF COMMUNITY SERVICE.

# Guru Tegh Bahadur

(1621 - 1675)

*Theekar Fore Dilees Sir, Prabh Par Kiyo Payan*
*Tegh Bahadur Si Kriya, Kari Na Kinhoo Aan*
*Tegh Bahadur Ke Chalat, Bhayo Jagat Main Sog*
*Hai Hai Hai Sab Jag Bhayo, Jai Jai Jai Sur Log*

He burst the bonds of mortal clay, and went on to the abode of God.
No one ever performed an act as noble as did Tegh Bahadur.
With the departure of Tegh Bahadur, the whole world was stricken with sorrow.
A wail of horror presided the earth, but there was a victor's welcome by the inhabitants of heaven.

GURU TEGH BAHADUR, THE NINTH SIKH GURU, WAS BORN IN APRIL 1621 IN AMRITSAR. HE WAS THE YOUNGEST SON OF GURU HAR GOBIND AND WAS ORIGINALLY NAMED TYAG MAL.
TYAG MAL LEARNED GURMUKHI, HINDI AND SANSKRIT FROM BHAI GURDAS, WHILE BABA BUDDHA TRAINED HIM IN ARCHERY AND HORSEMANSHIP. HE MASTERED SWORDSMANSHIP UNDER HIS FATHER'S GUIDANCE.
HINDI
GURMUKHI
SANSKRIT
AT ELEVEN, TYAG MAL MARRIED MATA GUJRI AT KARTARPUR. THEY HAD A SON, GOBIND RAI.
AT THIRTEEN, HE FOUGHT ALONGSIDE HIS FATHER AGAINST PAINDE KHAN. IMPRESSED BY HIS COURAGE, GURU HAR GOBIND NAMED HIM TEGH BAHADUR, OR 'BRAVE SWORDSMAN'.

AFTER HIS BROTHER GURDITTA'S SUDDEN DEMISE, TEGH BAHADUR MOVED TO BAKALA WITH HIS WIFE AND MOTHER. RENOUNCING WORLDLY PLEASURES, HE SPENT TWO DECADES IN SECLUSION, FOCUSSING ON MEDITATION, TAKING CARE OF HIS FAMILY AND ENGAGING IN CHARITY.
AFTER THE DEATH OF GURU HAR KRISHAN, EVERYONE WAS CONCERNED ABOUT WHO WOULD BECOME THE NEXT GURU.
GURU HAR KRISHAN HAS LEFT US. BEFORE PASSING, HE UTTERED THE WORDS, 'BABA BAKALA'. WHAT DO YOU THINK HE MEANT?
HE MEANT OUR NEXT GURU IS AN ELDER WHO LIVES IN BAKALA.
SEVERAL RELATIVES OF THE LATE GURU VIED FOR THE POSITION. DHIR MAL, A NEPHEW OF TEGH BAHADUR, WAS THE MOST INFLUENTIAL OF THEM ALL.
AROUND THIS TIME, A PROSPEROUS SIKH TRADER, MAKHAN SHAH, FOUND HIMSELF IN THE MIDDLE OF A STORM AT SEA.
GURU-JI, SAVE US FROM THIS STORM AND I'LL OFFER YOU FIVE HUNDRED GOLD COINS.

SOON, THE STORM CALMED AND MAKHAN SHAH RETURNED HOME SAFELY.
GRATEFUL FOR HIS SAFE RETURN, MAKHAN SHAH TRAVELLED TO BAKALA TO MEET THE NEW GURU. THERE, HE FOUND MANY WHO CLAIMED TO BE THE GURU. TO TEST THEM, HE VISITED EACHONE AND OFFERED THEM TWO GOLD COINS.
I AM THE GURU!
NO, I AM. LOOK NO FURTHER!
NONSENSE! THE COINS ARE MINE. I AM DHIR MAL. THE LEADERSHIP LEGITIMATELY BELONGS TO ME.
EACH SELF-PROCLAIMED GURU GRABBED THE COINS OFFERED BY MAKHAN SINGH, UNAWARE OF THE VOW HE HAD MADE, TO OFFER FIVE HUNDRED COINS TO THE GURU FOR SAVING HIS LIFE.
NONE OF THESE MEN IS THE TRUE GURU. I'VE HEARD PEOPLE SPEAK ABOUT TEGH BAHADUR. EVEN THOUGH HE DOESN'T CLAIM TO BE THE GURU, LET ME VISIT HIM TOO.
MAKHAN SHAH WENT TO TEGH BAHADUR'S HOUSE AND OFFERED HIM TWO GOLD COINS.
MAKHAN SHAH, YOU PROMISED TO GIVE FIVE HUNDRED COINS. WHERE ARE THE REST?
I HAVE FOUND THE TRUE GURU! TEGH BAHADUR IS OUR GURU!
HEARING THIS, MANY PEOPLE FLOCKED TO MAKE OFFERINGS AND SEEK BLESSINGS FROM THEIR NEW GURU.

UNHAPPY WITH THE TURN OF EVENTS, DHIR MAL AND HIS FOLLOWERS PLOTTED TO KILL GURU TEGH BAHADUR. IN THE MIDDLE OF THE NIGHT, THEY SNEAKED INTO HIS HOUSE.
SHIHAN, SHOOT HIM AND TAKE THE OFFERING!
SHIHAN FIRED, BUT LUCKILY, THE BULLET ONLY GRAZED THE GURU'S ARM. THEY RANSACKED THE HOUSE AND TOOK WHATEVER THEY COULD FIND.
WHEN MAKHAN SHAH HEARD OF THE INCIDENT, HE COMPELLED DHIR MAL AND HIS MEN TO APOLOGISE AND RETURN THE STOLEN GOODS.
GURU-JI, I AM ASHAMED OF MYSELF FOR HAVING CAUSED YOU HARM. PLEASE FORGIVE ME.
MEN OFTEN COMMIT EVIL DEEDS IN ANGER. MY DEAR NEPHEW, I HOPE YOU NEVER LET ANGER LEAD YOU TO SUCH ACTIONS AGAIN.
GURU TEGH BAHADUR LEFT BAKALA TO SPREAD THE SIKH IDEOLOGY. WHEN HE REACHED THE HARMANDIR SAHIB, HE FOUND THAT ALL THE DOORS WERE SHUT.
THESE PRIESTS ARE BLINDED BY THEIR GREED. YET, GOD IS OMNIPRESENT. I SHALL PAY MY RESPECTS FROM THIS SPOT.
FOLLOWING GURU HAR GOBIND'S DEPARTURE FROM AMRITSAR, THE SODHI FAMILY HAD ASSUMED CONTROL OVER THE GURUDWARA. THEY SHUT ALL THE DOORS WHEN THEY HEARD OF THE GURU'S ARRIVAL.

DISHEARTENED BY THE POLITICS IN AMRITSAR, GURU TEGH BAHADUR SOUGHT SOLACE IN A DISTANT LAND, WHERE HE LAID THE FOUNDATION OF THE CITY OF ANANDPUR SAHIB.
CONTINUING THE LEGACY OF GURU NANAK DEV, GURU TEGH BAHADUR BECAME THE SECOND GURU TO UNDERTAKE A TRANSFORMATIVE JOURNEY, CARRYING HIS MESSAGE ACROSS INDIA. WHEREVER HE HALTED, HE BUILT WELLS AND ESTABLISHED FREE KITCHENS.
THOUGH AURANGZEB ACKNOWLEDGED THE DIVINITY OF THE GURUS, HE VIEWED THE RISE OF SIKHISM WITH APPREHENSION. THOSE WHO RESISTEDCONVERSION TO ISLAM WERE ARRESTED.
IN AURANGZEB'S EYES, GURU TEGH BAHADUR WAS A THREAT. HE ORDERED HIS ARREST AND SENTENCED HIM TO DEATH. BUT RAJA RAM SINGH OF JAIPUR PLEADED FOR CLEMENCY ON HIS BEHALF AND PERSUADED AURANGZEB TO FREE THE GURU.
SOON AFTER HIS RELEASE, A FIFTEEN-MEMBER GROUP OF PROMINENT KASHMIRI PANDITS ARRIVED AT ANANDPUR SAHIB.
GURU-JI, WE NEED YOUR HELP. THE EMPEROR IS FORCING US TO CHOOSE BETWEEN CONVERTING TO ISLAM AND DEATH.
TELL AURANGZEB THAT IF HE SUCCEEDS IN CONVERTING TEGH BAHADUR, ALL THE HINDUS IN THE COUNTRY WILL EMBRACE ISLAM. BUT IF HE FAILS TO DO SO, HE MUST RETRACT HIS POLICY OF FORCED CONVERSION.

GURU TEGH BAHADUR WAS ARRESTED FOR SUPPORTING THE KASHMIRI PANDITS.
ANTICIPATING HIS FATE, GURU TEGH BAHADUR APPOINTED HIS YOUNG SON, GOBIND RAI, AS HIS SUCCESSOR.
IN NOVEMBER 1675, GURU TEGH BAHADUR WAS IMPRISONED IN A POLICE STATION AT CHANDNI CHOWK.
SO, WHEN ARE YOU CONVERTING TO ISLAM? REFUSAL WILL RESULT IN YOUR EXECUTION.
EVERY INDIVIDUAL HAS THE RIGHT TO CHOOSE THEIR RELIGION. FORCING A RELIGION ON OTHERS IS UNJUST. I BELIEVE MY FAITH IS JUST AS VALID AS ISLAM, SO I SEE NO REASON TO CHANGE IT.
AS FOR DEATH, I EMBRACE IT WILLINGLY, TO UPHOLD THE TEACHINGS OF MY GURUS.
TO WEAKEN THE GURU'S RESOLVE, THE EMPEROR SUBJECTED HIS DISCIPLES—BHAI MATI DAS, BHAI SATI DAS AND BHAI DYAL DAS—TO GRUESOME TORTURE IN FRONT OF HIM. BHAI MATI DAS WAS SAWED IN HALF. BHAI SATI DAS WAS BURNED ALIVE, WHILE BHAI DYAL DAS WAS BOILED ALIVE IN A CAULDRON.
AND NOW IT'S YOUR TURN! DO YOU WISH TO RECONSIDER YOUR DECISION?
MY FOLLOWERS REJECTED CONVERSION AND FACED DEATH. THEIR SACRIFICE ONLY STRENGTHENS MY RESOLVE. I WILL GO TO MY WAHEGURU, SETTING AN EXAMPLE BY STANDING FIRM FOR RIGHTEOUSNESS.

ON THE AFTERNOON OF 24 NOVEMBER 1675, GURU TEGH BAHADUR WAS BEHEADED.
THE MUGHALS REFUSED TO GIVE THE GURU'S BODY TO HIS DISCIPLES. THE BODY AND SEVERED HEAD LAY AT THE CROSSING OF CHANDNI CHOWK, AND NO ONE WAS ALLOWED TO APPROACH.
A TERRIBLE STORM ENGULFED DELHI THAT DAY, AND WHEN IT SUBSIDED, GURU TEGH BAHADUR'S BODY AND SEVERED HEAD HAD VANISHED.
HOW DID THEY DISAPPEAR?
PERHAPS THE GURU HAS RISEN UP TO HEAVEN!
I MUST DELIVER GURU-JI'S HEAD TO ANANDPUR TO HIS FAMILY.
JAITA, A COURAGEOUS SIKH, TRANSPORTED GURU TEGH BAHADUR'S SEVERED HEAD TO ANANDPUR UNDER COVER OF THE STORM.
MY SON! MY SON! I WISH I HAD NOT LIVED TO SEE THIS DREADFUL DAY!
RANGHRETA, GURU KA BETA!
RANGHRETA MEANT 'UNTOUCHABLE'. DESPITE SOCIETAL BARRIERS, GOBIND RAI EMBRACED JAITA, NAMING ALL UNTOUCHABLES AS THE GURU'S SONS.

LAKHI SHAH VANJARA, A TRADER, ALSO TOOK ADVANTAGE OF THE STORM. HE HID GURU TEGH BAHADUR'S HEADLESS BODY IN A COTTON CART AND TOOK IT TO HIS HUT. HECREMATED IT BY SETTING HIS HUT ON FIRE SO THAT THE EMPEROR WOULD NOT FIND OUT.
ACROSS COMMUNITIES, PEOPLE MOURNED GURU TEGH BAHADUR'S MARTYRDOM.

GURU TEGH BAHADUR'S MARTYRDOM RESHAPED SIKH HISTORY, INSPIRING A COMMUNITY TO RESIST TYRANNY.
GURU TEGH BAHADUR IS RIGHTFULLY HAILED AS A SAVIOUR, EARNING THE REVERED TITLE OF 'HIND DI CHAADAR'.

# Guru Gobind Singh

(1666 - 1708)

*Chirion Se Main Baaz Turaun, Tabe Gobind Singh Naam Kahaun*
*Gidderon Se Main Sher Banaun, Tabe Gobind Singh Naam Kahaun*
*Nichon Se Main Ucch Banaun, Tabe Gobind Singh Naam Kahaun*
*Sawa Lakh Se Ek Laraun, Tabe Gobind Singh Naam Kahaun*

It is when I make sparrows fight hawks that I am called Gobind Singh.
It is when I make lions out of wolves that I am called Gobind Singh.
It is when I make a lowly rise that I am called Gobind Singh.
It is when I make one fight a hundred thousand that I am called Gobind Singh.

EVERY ONCE IN A WHILE, AN EXCEPTIONAL SOUL RISES TO DEFEND HUMANITY AGAINST TYRANNY. ONE SUCH SOUL WAS GURU GOBIND SINGH.
BORN IN 1666 IN PATNA SAHIB, BIHAR, HE WAS THE SON OF GURU TEGH BAHADUR AND MATA GUJRI.
IN 1675, NINE-YEAR-OLD GOBIND RAI WAS PLAYING WITH HIS FRIENDS WHEN HIS MOTHER SUMMONED HIM TO HEAR A DEVASTATING NEWS.
SON, YOUR FATHER, GURU TEGH BAHADUR, WAS BRUTALLY TORTURED AND BEHEADED IN DELHI. DO NOT LOSE HEART; HE DIED A HERO'S DEATH, FIGHTING FOR HIS PEOPLE AND FAITH.
ON 24 NOVEMBER 1675, FOLLOWING HIS FATHER'S CREMATION, GOBIND RAI WAS ANOINTED AS GURU GOBIND.
GURU GOBIND SINGH ADORNED HIMSELF WITH A KALGI (A FEATHERED BROOCH WORN ON THE TURBAN) AND A ROYAL ATTIRE. HE WAS ARMED WITH A SWORD, A QUIVER OF ARROWS, AND A SHIELD. A WHITE FALCON SAT PERCHED ON HIS HAND, WHICH EARNED HIM THE TITLE 'MASTER OF THE WHITE HAWK'.
THE GURU TRAINED IN VARIOUS MARTIAL ARTS AND WAS WELL-VERSED IN MULTIPLE LANGUAGES AND SUBJECTS.

IN 1677, GURU GOBIND MARRIED SUNDARI. HE HAD FOUR SONS—AJIT SINGH, JUJHAR SINGH, ZORAWAR SINGH AND FATEH SINGH.
GURU GOBIND SINGH ESTABLISHED PAONTA SAHIB ON THE YAMUNA'S BANKS, WHERE HE COMPOSED POEMS AND HYMNS ADVOCATING LOVE AND PEACE. HE EMPHASISED ETHICAL CONDUCT AND BELIEF IN ONE GOD WHILE NURTURING A RICH LITERARY CULTURE. HE ORGANISED POETRY CONTESTS, REWARDED TALENT AND ENCOURAGED THE TRANSLATION OF SANSKRIT TEXTS BY DISTINGUISHED POETS IN HIS COURT.
GURU GOBIND SAW THE NEED TO TRAIN THE SIKHS IN SELF-DEFENCE DUE TO THE ESCALATING CONFLICT WITH THE MUGHALS.
WHEN PEACEFUL METHODS FAIL TO SWAY THE WICKED, IT BECOMES JUST TO WIELD THE SWORD IN DEFENCE OF OUR HONOUR.
WHEN SIKH SOLDIERS DOUBTED THEIR ABILITY TO FIGHT THE MUGHALS, GURU GOBIND IGNITED THEIR SPIRITS WITH PURPOSE AND UNWAVERING RESOLVE.
I WILL TURN SPARROWS INTO HAWKS. OUR BATTLE CRY WILL BE 'SAT SRI AKAL', MEANING GOD IS THE ULTIMATE TRUTH! EVERYONE, REPEAT AFTER ME, 'BOLE SO NIHAAL, SAT SRI AKAL'!
BOLE SO NIHAAL, SAT SRI AKAL!

GURU GOBIND RESOLVED TO TRAIN A COMMUNITY OF WARRIORS. ON BAISAKHI, HE ADDRESSED 80,000 FOLLOWERS. RAISING HIS GLEAMING SWORD, HE CALLED OUT TO THE SIKHS.
I WANT ONE HEAD. IS THERE ANYONE HERE WHO CAN OFFER ME HIS HEAD IN THE NAME OF RIGHTEOUSNESS?
EVERYONE WAS TAKEN ABACK BY THE GURU'S REQUEST. NO SIKH VOLUNTEERED INITIALLY. IT WAS ONLY ON THE THIRD CALL THAT DAYA RAM, A KHATRI FROM LAHORE, BROKE THE SILENCE.
MURMUR MURMUR
MURMUR MURMUR
GURU-JI, MY HEAD IS AT YOUR SERVICE!
THE GURU AND DAYA RAM ENTERED THE TENT. A THUD OF THE SWORD WAS HEARD. WHEN THE GURU EMERGED, HE WAS ALONE, HIS SWORD STAINED WITH BLOOD. 'ANOTHER HEAD,' HE CALLED, AND DHARAM DAS, A JAT FROM DELHI, STEPPED FORWARD.
MY HEAD IS AT YOUR DISPOSAL, GURU-JI!
GURU GOBIND TOOK HIM INTO THE TENT AS WELL. ONCE AGAIN, THE THUD RANG OUT FROM THE TENT AND THE GURU EMERGED ALONE WITH HIS BLOOD-STAINED SWORD. NEXT, MOHKAM CHAND, A TAILOR FROM THE WEST COAST, STEPPED FORWARD. HIMMAT CHAND, A COOK FROM JAGANNATH PURI, AND SAHIB CHAND, A BARBER FROM BIDAR, ALL VOLUNTEERED AS THE GURU CONTINUED TO ASK FOR HEADS.

FINALLY, GURU GOBIND SINGH BROUGHT OUT THE FIVE VOLUNTEERS, ALIVE AND IN NEW GARMENTS.
I PRESENT TO YOU THE PANJ PYARE, MY FIVE BELOVED ONES!
THE CROWD THAT STAYED TILL THE END REALISED THAT THEIR GURU WAS TESTING THEIR LOYALTY THROUGH THE SWORD RITUAL. THEY REGRETTED DOUBTING HIM.
GURU GOBIND FILLED A VESSEL WITH SOME WATER, ADDED SUGAR AND STIRRED IT WITH A DOUBLE-EDGED DAGGER, CALLED THE KHANDA.
DRINK THIS SWEET WATER, AMRIT. YOU ARE NOW SINGHS, MEANING LIONS. YOU MUST FOLLOW THE FIVE KS. THE FIRST IS KESH (HAIR)—NEVER CUT YOUR HAIR OR BEARD. NEXT IS THE KANGHA (A WOODEN COMB)—ALWAYS CARRY IT WITH YOU. THE THIRD IS THE KADA (A STEEL BRACELET).
FOURTH IS THE KIRPAN (A DAGGER) FOR DEFENCE. AND FINALLY, KACCHA (THE SOLDIERS' BREECHES) TO ALWAYS BE READY FOR BATTLE. REMEMBER, AS MY KHALSA, NEVER HARM THE WEAK, NEVER HARM WOMEN AND REGARD ALL HUMANS AS BROTHERS, REGARDLESS OF CASTE OR CREED.
THE PANJ PYARE COME FROM DIFFERENT BACKGROUNDS, UNITED AS ONE. YOU WILL WEAR THE FIVE KS AND PROTECT THE WEAK.
KADA
KESH
KANGHA
KACCHA
KIRPAN
THUS, HE ANOINTED THE PANJ PYARE, FORMING A NEW COMMUNITY—THE KHALSA OR THE PURE. AT GURU GOBIND'S REQUEST, THE PANJ PYARE WENT ON TO ANOINT HIM, DESPITE HIS ROLE AS THE GURU. IN THIS NEW ORDER, THERE WOULD BE NO DISTINCTION BETWEEN THE GURU AND THE FIVE.
THE KHALSA IS THE GURU, AND THE GURU IS THE KHALSA!
WAHE GURU-JI KA KHALSA, WAHE GURU-JI KI FATEH! KHALSA BELONGS TO GOD, AND ALL TRIUMPHS ARE IN HIS NAME.

ONE DAY, GURU GOBIND SINGH TIED A TIGER SKIN THAT HE HAD BEEN GIFTED ONTO A DONKEY AND SET IT LOOSE. MISTAKING IT FOR A REAL TIGER, THE VILLAGERS FLED IN TERROR.
I DRAPED THE SKIN ON THE DONKEY TO TEACH YOU A LESSON. REMEMBER THIS: THE UNIFORM HOLDS POWER. AS LONG AS THE DONKEY WORE THE TIGER SKIN, YOU FEARED IT. BUT ONCE THE SKIN WAS REMOVED, YOU SAW IT FOR WHAT IT WAS—A DONKEY.
I'VE MADE THE SINGH UNIFORM. WEAR IT, FEEL STRONG LIKE A LION AND STAND AGAINST EVIL. WITHOUT IT, BOUND BY THE CASTE SYSTEM, YOU'LL FEEL WEAK.
AFTER THAT DAY, THE MINDS OF THOSE WHO HAD BEEN STILL WARY WERE INFUSED WITH A NEW SPIRIT. WITHIN TWO WEEKS, MORE THAN 80,000 FOLLOWERS HAD BEEN BAPTISED.
IN 1704, ALARMED BY THE GROWING STRENGTH OF THE SIKH REGIMENT, EMPEROR AURANGZEB, ALONGSIDE THE RAJAS AND GOVERNORS OF LAHORE AND SIRHIND, UNITED FORCES TO DISMANTLE GURU GOBIND SINGH'S ARMY AND CAPTURE HIM.
GURU-JI, THE MUGHAL ARMY HAS SURROUNDED THE FORT FROM ALL SIDES!
SHUT THE GATES AND TELL OUR SOLDIERS TO MAINTAIN THE ENEMY AT A DISTANCE WITH THE HELP OF CANNONBALLS.
SIKH SOLDIERS JUMPED FROM THE WALLS OF THE FORT AND FOUGHT FIERCELY TO PROTECT THEIR HOME. THEIR WAR CRIES ECHOED BEYOND THE BATTLEFIELD.
SEEING HOW THEIR WELL-TRAINED SOLDIERS WERE UNABLE TO DEFEAT THE SIKH ARMY, THE MUGHAL ARMY USED WAR ELEPHANTS TO CHARGE THE MAIN GATE OF THE FORT.
BOLE SO NIHAAL, SAT SRI AKAL!
BOLE SO NIHAAL, SAT SRI AKAL!
BOLE SO NIHAAL, SAT SRI AKAL!

AT THE END OF THE SECOND DAY OF FIGHTING, THE SIKH SOLDIERS BROUGHT BHAI KANHAIYA, A LOCAL SIKH WHO HAD BEEN OFFERING WATER TO THE WOUNDED ENEMY SOLDIERS.
GURU-JI, BHAI KANHAIYA HAS BEEN OFFERING WATER TO THE WOUNDED ENEMY SOLDIERS!
GURU-JI, I HAVE BEEN GIVING WATER TO EVERYONE ON THE BATTLEFIELD. I CANNOT DIFFERENTIATE BETWEEN THE SIKHS, THE HINDUS AND THE MUSLIMS. I SEE EVERYONE AS GOD'S CREATION.
YOU ARE DOING A NOBLE DEED. YOU HAVE TRULY UNDERSTOOD THE TEACHINGS OF YOUR GURUS. YOU ARE MY TRUE SIKH!
GURU GOBIND SINGH GAVE BHAI KANHAIYA BANDAGES AND MEDICINES AND BLESSED HIM TO CONTINUE SERVING THE WOUNDED, REGARDLESS OF THEIR RELIGION.
ON THE THIRD DAY, REALISING THE SIKHS' FIERCENESS, THE MUGHAL ARMY WITHDREW TO A SAFE DISTANCE. THEY PLANNED TO CUT OFF ALL SUPPLIES TO THE FORT TO STARVE THE SIKHS TO DEATH.
GURU-JI, THE MUGHALS HAVE RETREATED, BUT WE HAVE RUN OUT OF FOOD AND SUPPLIES. HOW WILL WE FEED OUR SOLDIERS? WE WILL ALL DIE OF HUNGER SOON.
THE MUGHALS LAID SIEGE TO ANANDPUR FORT FOR MONTHS. THE SIKHS' COURAGE AND STRENGTH IN FACE OF MANY HARDSHIPS BEGAN TO WEAR DOWN THE MUGHAL ARMY. FINALLY, THE EMPEROR SENT A LETTER TO GURU GOBIND SINGH.
If you agree to leave Anandpur Fort you will not be attacked or followed and can go wherever you like in the country.
I promise you safe passage out of the city and grant you permission to return to Anandpur at a later time.
GURU GOBIND SINGH, UNSURE OF THE PROMISE BUT LOW ON SUPPLIES, HAD TO AGREE. ON 20 DECEMBER 1704, IN HEAVY RAIN AND FIERCE WINDS, HE LEFT ANANDPUR FORT WITH HIS FAMILY AND FOUR HUNDRED SOLDIERS.
AS SOON AS THE SIKHS LEFT THE FORT, THE MUGHAL ARMY AMBUSHED THEM AT THE SIRSA RIVER BANK. CAUGHT OFF GUARD, THE SIKHS FOUGHT BRAVELY, BUT MANY LOST THEIR LIVES.
GURU-JI, WE HAVE BEEN BETRAYED! THE MUGHALS DID NOT KEEP THEIR PROMISE!
QUICKLY HELP THE WOMEN AND CHILDREN TO THE OTHER SIDE OF THE RIVER!

AMIDST THE COLD AND THE INTENSE COMBAT, THE SIKHS WERE OVERCOME WITH CONFUSION AND BEWILDERMENT. IN THE CHAOS, THE GURU'S MOTHER, MATA GUJRI AND HIS TWO YOUNGER SONS WERE SEPARATED FROM THE FAMILY.
GURU GOBIND SINGH MANAGED TO CROSS THE RIVER ONLY TO FIND THAT HE WAS LEFT WITH JUST TWO OF HIS SONS, THE PANJ PYARE AND ONLY THIRTY-FIVE OF HIS SOLDIERS.
ONLY FORTY-THREE OF THEM WERE LEFT, YET GURU GOBIND SINGH REFUSED TO SURRENDER. THEY SOUGHT REFUGE IN A MUD BUILDING IN CHAMKAUR, TURNING IT INTO A MAKESHIFT FORT.
BY NIGHTFALL, THE MUGHAL ARMY HAD SURROUNDED THE FORTRESS WITH INSTRUCTIONS TO CAPTURE THE GURU ALIVE.
THE SIKH SOLDIERS FOUGHT VALIANTLY, MANY LAID DOWN THEIR LIVES.

FATHER, WE WILL GO OUT AND HELP OUR SOLDIERS!
NO, GURU-JI, DO NOT GIVE PERMISSION. WE CANNOT RISK YOUR SONS' LIVES!
ALL OF YOU ARE MY SONS! I WILL PROUDLY LOSE MY SONS FOR A RIGHTEOUS CAUSE! GO, MY SONS! FIGHT AND DIE A TRUE WARRIOR!
AFTER A WHILE...
GURU-JI, WE LOST BOTH YOUR SONS. WE HAVE NO CHOICE BUT TO SURRENDER!
MY SON'S PHYSIQUE IS LIKE YOURS. WE COULD DRESS HIM AS YOU TO FOOL THE ENEMY. WHILE HE IS OUT FIGHTING, YOU HAVE TO MAKE AN ESCAPE TO CHAMKAUR.
GURU GOBIND SINGH RELUCTANTLY AGREED, DISGUISING A YOUNG SIKH AS HIMSELF. HE PUT HIS KALGI ON THE TURBAN OF THE YOUNG SIKH. DRESSED IN THE SAME ATTIRE AS THE GURU'S, NO ONE COULD TELL THEM APART.
THE YOUNG SIKH WENT TO FACE THE ENEMY WHILE THE GURU ESCAPED.
WE HAVE KILLED THE GURU! VICTORY IS OURS!

AMIDST MUGHAL CELEBRATIONS, GURU GOBIND SINGH FLEES THROUGH THE MACHIWARA FOREST WITH HIS COMPANIONS BHAI DAYA SINGH, BHAI MAAN SINGH AND BHAI DHARAM SINGH. UNFORTUNATELY, GURU GOBIND SINGH WAS SEPARATED FROM THEM. HE LAY UNDER A TREE, AWAITING THEM.
MEANWHILE, MATA GUJRI AND GURU GOBIND SINGH'S SONS, BABA ZORAVER SINGH AND BABA FATEH SINGH, HAD SOUGHT REFUGE WITH GANGU, THE FAMILY'S COOK. UNDER THE COVER OF NIGHT, GANGU STOLE FROM THEM. WHEN ACCUSED, HE DENIED IT AND BETRAYED THEM TO THE VILLAGE HEADMAN, WHO IN TURN ALERTED THE MUGHALS, SEALING THEIR FATE.
MATA GUJRI, BABA ZORAVER SINGH AND BABA FATEH SINGH WERE TAKEN TO THE WAZIR KHAN, GOVERNOR OF SIRHIND, WHO ORDERED THEM TO BE CONFINED IN A TOWER.
IN CONFINEMENT, MATA GUJRI AND HER GRANDSONS ENDURED A COLD, HARSH NIGHT WITHOUT FOOD OR WATER.
THE NEXT MORNING...
DEAR SONS, YOU WILL BE TAKEN TO WAZIR KHAN'S COURT. WHILE YOU ARE THERE, DO NOT FORGET YOUR VOW TO YOUR GOD AND YOUR FATHER.

CONVERT TO ISLAM AND LIVE, OR FACE DEATH LIKE YOUR FATHER! YOU HAVE THE NIGHT TO DECIDE. IF YOU AGREE, YOU WILL RECEIVE MANY GIFTS AND A COMFORTABLE LIFE. IF NOT, YOU WILL BE BRICKED ALIVE!
WE SHALL PROUDLY GIVE OUR LIVES JUST LIKE OUR FATHER DID! WAHE GURU-JI KA KHALSA, WAHE GURU-JI KI FATEH! NO MATTER HOW MANY TIMES YOU ASK, OUR ANSWER WILL REMAIN THE SAME.
WAZIR KHAN, EXTREMELY ANNOYED BY THEIR CONFIDENCE, ASKED WHAT THEY WOULD DO WITH THEIR LIVES IF HE SET THEM FREE.
WE SHALL GATHER THE SINGHS AND FIGHT AGAINST TYRANNY UNTIL IT IS FINISHED, OR WE SHALL DIE FIGHTING IT!
I HAVE DECIDED NOT TO WAIT UNTIL THE MORNING. YOU SHALL MEET YOUR FATE RIGHT NOW! BOTH OF YOU WILL BE BRICKED ALIVE!
ON 27 DECEMBER 1704, THE CHOTTE SAHIBZADAS, AGED SEVEN AND FIVE, WERE BRICKED ALIVE. THEIR UNWAVERING FAITH MARKED A DEFEAT FOR THE GOVERNOR.
UPON HEARING THE NEWS OF HER GRANDCHILDREN, MATA GUJRI CALLED OUT TO WAHE GURU ONE LAST TIME AND PASSED AWAY.
IN THE MEANTIME, AT THE COURT OF THE EMPEROR, THE MUGHAL GENERAL WAS INFORMED OF THE TRICK PLAYED ON HIM AND HIS ARMY—THE GURU WAS STILL ALIVE. THEY SET OUT IN LARGE FORCES IN SEARCH OF HIM.

AFTER REUNITING WITH HIS THREE COMPANIONS, GURU GOBIND SINGH MET TWO DEVOTED PATHANS, NABI KHAN AND GANI KHAN. LEARNING OF THE GURU'S HIDING PLACE, THEY HAD BROUGHT FOOD AND CLOTHES.
DISGUISING THE GURU AS A PIR IN BLUE GARMENTS, THEY CARRIED HIM ON A BENCH THROUGH THE FOREST, PAST MACHIWARA AND TO THE VILLAGE OF GHULAL.
ON ARRIVING, GURU GOBIND SINGH HEARD THE TERRIBLE NEWS.
GURU-JI, WE HAVE LOST ALL FOUR OF YOUR SONS AND YOUR MOTHER IS DEAD AS WELL.
HMM ... I HAVE LOST FOUR SONS, BUT A HUNDRED THOUSAND OF MY SIKH SONS ARE STILL ALIVE!
DESPITE HIS BRAVE DEMEANOUR, GURU GOBIND SINGH WAS DEEPLY TROUBLED. HE WROTE A LONG LETTER TO EMPEROR AURANGZEB CALLED THE 'ZAFARNAMA' (A DECLARATION OF VICTORY), CONTAINING A HUNDRED AND ELEVEN VERSES.
You are the king of kings, oh, fortunate Aurangzeb. You are a clever administrator and a good horseman. With the help of your intelligence and the sword, you have become the master. You are the master of the country, and its wealth. Though you are the king of kings, you are far from righteousness and justice.
If God is friendly, what can the enemy do? The enemy may try to give a thousand blows, but he cannot harm even one hair.
IN HIS VERSES, GURU GOBIND SINGH EXPOSED THE EMPEROR'S BROKEN OATHS MADE IN GOD'S NAME. HE POINTED OUT THAT, DESPITE THEIR DECEIT, THEY FAILED TO CAPTURE THE GURU. THE LETTER AIMED TO CONVEY GURU GOBIND SINGH'S MORAL VICTORY, EVEN AFTER LOSING HIS SONS, MOTHER, SOLDIERS AND FORTS.

A FEW DAYS LATER, THE MUGHAL ARMY, STILL IN SEARCH OF GURU GOBIND SINGH, FINALLY MET UP WITH HIM.
A FIERCE BATTLE WAS FOUGHT, BUT THE MUGHALS WERE DEFEATED AND MADE TO RETREAT.
THIS WAS GURU GOBIND SINGH'S LAST BATTLE. HE THEN MOVED TO SABO-KI-TALWANDI, LATER KNOWN AS DAMDAMA SAHIB. SIKH FOLLOWERS MADE IT AN ACTIVE CENTRE AS ANANDPUR SAHIB. AT SABO-KI-TALWANDI, THE GURU PREPARED COPIES OF THE 'GURU GRANTH SAHIB', WHICH WERE SENT TO MAJOR SIKH CENTRES.
MEANWHILE, AFTER READING THE 'ZAFARNAMA', THE EMPEROR'S PEACE OF MIND WAS MIGHTILY DISTURBED. HE HAD LOST THE ZEST TO FIGHT THE GURU. HE WROTE A LETTER TO HIS SONS AS WELL AS ONE TO THE GURU.
Allah was in my heart, but my blind eyes failed to see him. I do not know how I will be received in Allah's court. I have committed many sins, against his own loved children and I do not know what punishments will be awarded to me in return.
IN THE LETTER TO THE GURU, HE REQUESTED TO MEET HIM PERSONALLY, IN ORDER TO SEEK REDEMPTION. HE WITHDREW ALL ORDERS AGAINST THE GURU TO ALLOW FOR HIS SAFE PASSAGE TO DELHI.
GURU GOBIND SINGH, INITIALLY RELUCTANT TO MEET THE EMPEROR, DECIDED TO GO TO DELHI. MIDWAY THROUGH HIS JOURNEY, HE RECEIVED NEWS OF THE EMPEROR'S DEATH. HE HAD SUCCUMBED TO THE PAIN CAUSED BY HIS DEEDS.

AFTER EMPEROR AURANGZEB'S DEATH, A FIGHT FOR THE THRONE LED HIS ELDEST SON, BAHADUR SHAH, TO SEEK THE GURU'S HELP AGAINST HIS BROTHER AZAM.
GURU GOBIND SINGH SENT A SQUAD LED BY BHAI DAYA SINGH TO JOIN BAHADUR SHAH NEAR MATHURA. THE GURU HIMSELF SET UP CAMP ON HIGH GROUND AND SHOT AN ARROW THAT KILLED AZAM. BAHADUR SHAH EMERGED VICTORIOUS AND SOON BECAME THE NEXT EMPEROR.
A FEW DAYS LATER, UNAWARE THAT GURU GOBIND SINGH WASTHE ONE WHO KILLED AZAM, BAHADUR SHAH SUMMONED BHAI DAYA SINGH.
BHAI DAYA SINGH, YOUR GURU HAD PROMISED TO COME AND HELP ME WIN THE BATTLE, BUT HE DID NOT COME.
IN A SPLIT SECOND, AN ARROW WITH A GOLDEN TIP LANDED AT THE EMPEROR'S FEET. IT RESEMBLED THE ONE THAT KILLED AZAM. GURU GOBIND SINGH'S ARROWS ALWAYS HAD GOLD TIPS, ALLOWING THE FAMILIES OF THE WOUNDED ENEMIES TO USE THE GOLD FOR THEIR LIVELIHOOD AFTER LOSING THEIR MEN IN BATTLE.
THIS IS MY GURU'S REPLY TO YOU! HE IS STILL WITH YOU, JUST AS HE WAS ON THE DAY OF THE BATTLE.
OH, THIS IS A MIRACLE! HOW DID HE SHOOT AN ARROW FROM SO FAR AND WITH SUCH PRECISION?

IN THE NEXT INSTANT, ANOTHER ARROW LODGED AT THE EXACT SAME PLACE NEAR THE EMPEROR'S FEET. A LETTER WAS ATTACHED TO THE ARROW.
Oh, great King! This is no miracle. This is the excellence of skill!
THE EMPEROR REALISED THAT GURU GOBIND SINGH COULD READ MINDS. HE INVITED THE GURU TO HIS COURT IN AGRA, RECOGNISING THAT HIS CONTRIBUTION HAD LED TO THEIR VICTORY IN BATTLE. FINALLY, YEARS OF ANIMOSITY BETWEEN THE MUGHAL EMPERORS AND THE GURUS CAME TO AN END.
SOON AFTER, GURU GOBIND SINGH LEFT FOR THE CITY OF NANDED IN MAHARASHTRA, AND SETTLED DOWN ON THE BANKS OF THE RIVER GODAVARI.
UPON LEARNING OF THE FRIENDSHIP BETWEEN THE EMPEROR AND THE GURU, WAZIR KHAN, FEARING PUNISHMENT FOR HIS PAST CRUELTIES, DISPATCHED ASSASSINS. THESE ASSAILANTS BRUTALLY ATTACKED THE GURU AT MIDNIGHT WHILE HE WAS SLEEPING.
AH! WHY ARE YOU ATTACKING ME? YOU HAVE COME, SURELY, WITH ORDERS NOT FROM YOUR EMPEROR.
WE HAVE BEEN GIVEN ORDERS TO KILL YOU, FOR IF WE DO NOT, YOU WILL GET OUR GOVERNOR, WAZIR KHAN, PROSECUTED.
BEFORE THE ASSASSINS COULD TAKE ANOTHER JAB AT GURU GOBIND SINGH, SIKHS CAME CHARGING IN AND KILLED THE ASSASSINS.

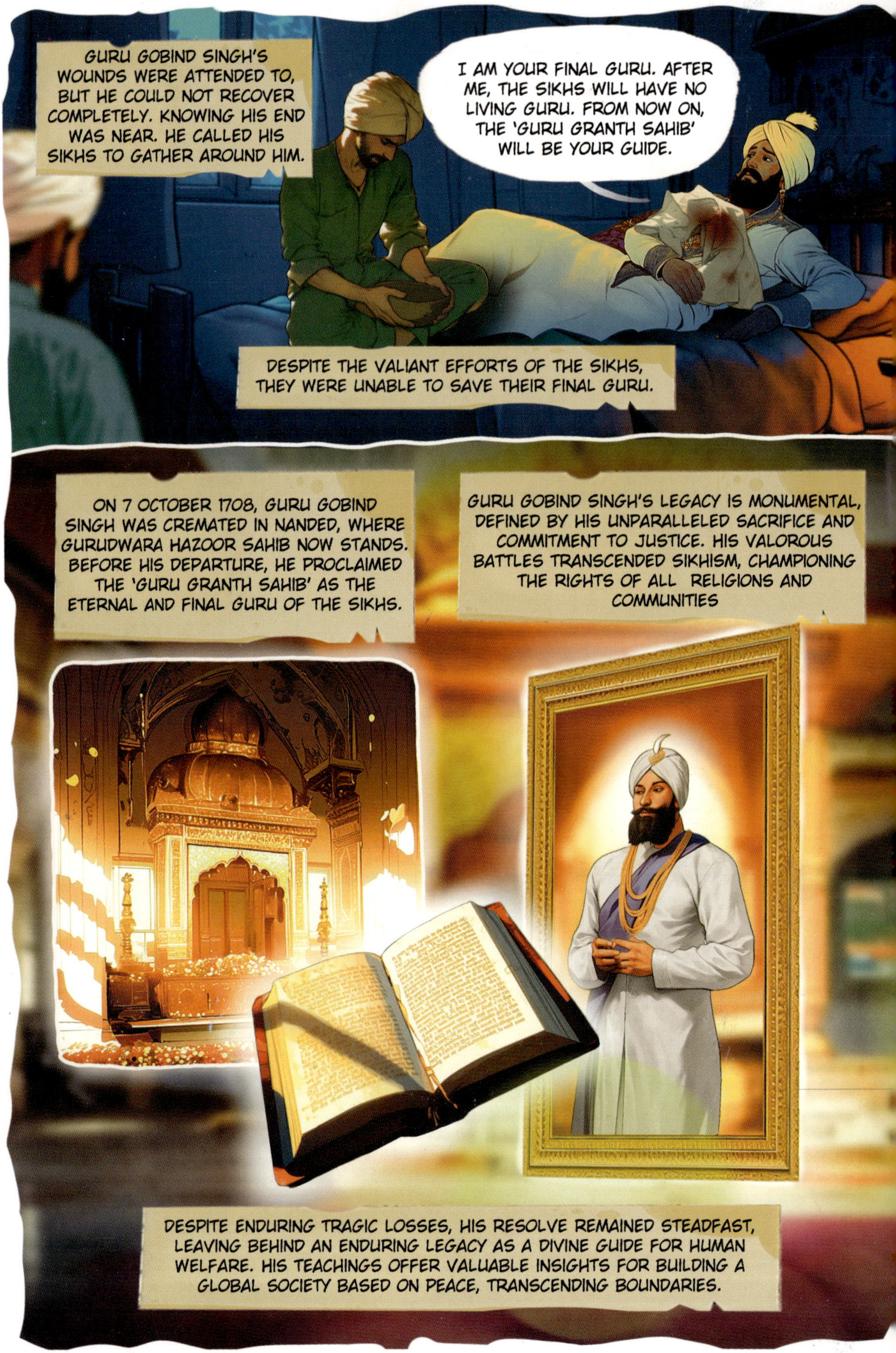
GURU GOBIND SINGH'S WOUNDS WERE ATTENDED TO, BUT HE COULD NOT RECOVER COMPLETELY. KNOWING HIS END WAS NEAR. HE CALLED HIS SIKHS TO GATHER AROUND HIM.
I AM YOUR FINAL GURU. AFTER ME, THE SIKHS WILL HAVE NO LIVING GURU. FROM NOW ON, THE 'GURU GRANTH SAHIB' WILL BE YOUR GUIDE.
DESPITE THE VALIANT EFFORTS OF THE SIKHS, THEY WERE UNABLE TO SAVE THEIR FINAL GURU.
ON 7 OCTOBER 1708, GURU GOBIND SINGH WAS CREMATED IN NANDED, WHERE GURUDWARA HAZOOR SAHIB NOW STANDS. BEFORE HIS DEPARTURE, HE PROCLAIMED THE 'GURU GRANTH SAHIB' AS THE ETERNAL AND FINAL GURU OF THE SIKHS.
GURU GOBIND SINGH'S LEGACY IS MONUMENTAL, DEFINED BY HIS UNPARALLELED SACRIFICE AND COMMITMENT TO JUSTICE. HIS VALOROUS BATTLES TRANSCENDED SIKHISM, CHAMPIONING THE RIGHTS OF ALL RELIGIONS AND COMMUNITIES
DESPITE ENDURING TRAGIC LOSSES, HIS RESOLVE REMAINED STEADFAST, LEAVING BEHIND AN ENDURING LEGACY AS A DIVINE GUIDE FOR HUMAN WELFARE. HIS TEACHINGS OFFER VALUABLE INSIGHTS FOR BUILDING A GLOBAL SOCIETY BASED ON PEACE, TRANSCENDING BOUNDARIES.